THE CULINARY ARTS INSTITUTE
has been developing, writing, and testing recipes since 1936. Its famous all-purpose cookery
guide—The American Woman's Cookbook—is
one of the ten best-selling cookbooks of all time.

Now the experts tell you how to can more than
thirty vegetables and fruits, create thirty fabu-
lous pickles and relishes, put up forty-five jellies, jams, and other preserves.

You'll discover how to make private-label frozen
dinners from your family's favorite recipes so
that you can have meals ready to pluck from
the freezer and serve in minutes. Your freezer
will become a treasure trove of colorful, nutri-
tious vegetables. You'll have meats, poultry,
game, fish, shellfish, and herbs ready and wait-
ing to do your culinary bidding. Sandwiches,
dairy products, and homemade baked goods
will always be conveniently at hand.

S0-ARS-839

THE CANNING AND FREEZING BOOK
was originally published by
Consolidated Book Publishers, Inc.

The CANNING

THE CANNING AND FREEZING BOOK

**Dee Munson
and the Culinary Arts Institute Staff:**

Helen Geist: Director
Sherrill Corley: Editor
Barbara MacDonald: Associate Editor
Ethel La Roche: Editorial Assistant
Ivanka Simatic: Recipe Tester
Edward Finnegan: Executive Editor
Charles Bozett: Art Director
Book coordinated by Laurel DiGangi

Illustrations by Diana Magnuson

AND FREEZING
Book

PUBLISHED BY POCKET BOOKS NEW YORK

THE CANNING AND FREEZING BOOK

Consolidated Book Publishers edition published 1975

POCKET BOOK edition published May, 1976

This POCKET BOOK edition includes every word contained in the original, higher-priced edition. It is printed from brand-new plates made from completely reset, clear, easy-to-read type.
POCKET BOOK editions are published by
POCKET BOOKS,
a division of Simon & Schuster, Inc.,
A GULF+WESTERN COMPANY
630 Fifth Avenue,
New York, N.Y. 10020.
Trademarks registered in the United States
and other countries.

Standard Book Number: 671-80434-0.
Library of Congress Catalog Card Number: 75-18757.

1276

ACKNOWLEDGMENTS

American Spice Trade Association
Fleischmann's Yeast
Fresh Bartlett Promotion Advisory Board
General Foods Kitchens
Kerr Glass Manufacturing Corporation (for the charts on pages 14-15, 29, 30, 38, 39, and 70)
Nectarine Administrative Committee
North American Blueberry Council
Sunkist Growers, Inc.

FOREWORD

There's a wonderful feeling that comes from putting up food—it's a feeling of accomplishment and security. You know that shelves and freezer are stocked with foods that you picked for their beauty, flavor, and freshness. You know that nothing but the best ingredients went into your efforts. And, even though it's hard to prove, you know that these foods taste better—just because you prepared them yourself! You'll save money by preserving your own food, too, *if* you shop wisely and follow procedures and recipes exactly.

This book will help you preserve food by canning, by pickling, and by freezing. All the basics are here. The instructions are simple and step by step—easy to follow for the beginner who wants the comfort of clear and explicit directions. The recipes are, to put it simply, the best! Freezer-owners will find ways to turn their appliance into a storehouse of home-prepared "convenience" foods, and even long-time canners and picklers will find new recipes here to add to treasured collections.

All information in this book and all processing times are based on the latest know-how and research from the United States Department of Agriculture. As more and more people start to preserve food at home and perhaps are slipshod about processing, the hazards of food safety have increased, so follow these times and these methods exactly. If you follow procedures, food preserving, especially canning, has no dangers. Short cuts and improper processing, timing, and packaging can produce food that isn't safe.

ALWAYS read the introductory material in each section BEFORE you begin to can, jelly, pickle, or freeze. Then read and follow the recipes exactly. Goodness will be yours.

CONTENTS

The
CANNING
AND
FREEZING
Book

CANNING

Canning has been a popular method of preserving foods since Nicholas Appert discovered that provisions could be cooked and sealed in containers to feed Napoleon's army.

Although the principles of canning used today are still basically the same as Appert's, our equipment and procedures are, thankfully, much more modern, convenient, and safe. Glass jars with easy-sealing lids, safe and easy-to-use pressure canners, thermostatically controlled burners, and sparkling, efficient kitchens make canning an activity many cooks choose for pleasure as well as to preserve food.

Canning is a two-step process. First the food is heated to temperatures high enough to kill the microorganisms that can cause spoilage. Then the food is sealed in containers so the microorganisms can't get back in. Microorganisms may be molds, yeasts, bacteria, or enzymes.

Enzymes are natural substances, found in foods, that affect color, flavor, and texture. Proper processing and temperatures can destroy enzyme activity. Molds and yeasts are usually deterred by heating food at boiling temperatures for a few minutes. Bacteria are more difficult to control, since there is such a variety of them and since some are resistant to heat. Proper containers, proper closures, and proper processing times will destroy harmful bacteria and guarantee good wholesome food.

APPROXIMATE YIELD OF CANNED

FOOD	FRESH
FRUITS	
*Apples	1 bu. (48 lb.)†
Apricots	1 bu. (50 lb.)
Berries, except strawberries	24-qt. crate
Cherries (as picked)	1 bu. (56 lb.)
*Peaches	1 bu. (48 lb.)
*Pears	1 bu. (50 lb.)
Pineapple	2 average
*Plums	1 bu. (56 lb.)
Strawberries	24-qt. crate
*Tomatoes	1 bu. (53 lb.)
VEGETABLES	
Asparagus	1 bu. (45 lb.)
Beans, lima (in pods)	1 bu. (32 lb.)
Beans, green	1 bu. (30 lb.)
Beets (without tops)	1 bu. (52 lb.)
Brussels sprouts	1 lb.
Carrots (without tops)	1 bu. (50 lb.)
Corn, sweet (in husks)	1 bu. (35 lb.)
Okra	1 bu. (26 lb.)
Peas, green (in pods)	1 bu. (30 lb.)
Spinach	1 bu. (18 lb.)
Squash, summer	1 bu. (40 lb.)
Sweet potatoes	1 bu. (55 lb.)

* 3 to 4 med. apples or pears per lb.
4 medium peaches or tomatoes per lb. 8 medium plums per lb.
† Legal weight of a bushel of fruits or vegetables varies from state to state. These are average weights.

FRUITS AND VEGETABLES FROM FRESH

CANNED	APPROX. AMT. NEEDED FOR 1 QT. JAR
16 to 20 qt.	2½ to 3 lbs.
20 to 24 qt.	2 to 2½ lbs.
12 to 18 qt.	1½ to 3 lbs.
22 to 32 qt.	2 to 2½ lbs.
18 to 24 qt.	2 to 3 lbs.
20 to 25 qt.	2 to 3 lbs.
1 qt.	
24 to 30 qt.	1½ to 2½ lbs.
12 to 16 qt.	
15 to 20 qt.	2½ to 3½ lbs.
11 qt.	2½ to 4½ lbs.
6 to 8 qt.	3 to 5 lbs.
15 to 20 qt.	1½ to 2½ lbs.
17 to 20 qt.	2 to 3½ lbs.
1 pint	
16 to 20 qt.	2 to 3 lbs.
8 to 9 qt.	3 to 6 lbs.
17 qt.	1½ lbs.
12 to 15 qt.	3 to 6 lbs.
6 to 9 qt.	2 to 6 lbs.
16 to 20 qt.	2 to 4 lbs.
18 to 22 qt.	2 to 3 lbs.

The greatest risk in home-canning of foods is botulism, a poison produced by bacteria (*Clostridium botulinum*) in a sealed jar. This poison can cause sickness, even death. The spores of this bacteria are destroyed when low-acid foods are correctly processed in a steam pressure canner in good working condition. This is why we recommend that all vegetables, except tomatoes, be processed in a pressure canner, and for the length of time given in the recipe. As a further precaution, *always* heat home-canned vegetables, meats, poultry and fish to boiling, then cover and boil 10 to 15 minutes *before* tasting or using. Spinach and corn should be boiled for 20 minutes. Stir them occasionally as they boil to distribute heat evenly throughout the vegetables. For safety tips, see page 42.

FOODS FOR CANNING

Select foods for canning carefully—pick them for perfection. Canning won't improve fruits and vegetables, it will only preserve them. So pick the best to preserve the best.

Select young and tender vegetables. Fruits and tomatoes should be firm and ripe, and all foods must be fresh. When fruits and vegetables leave the ground or tree they begin to lose freshness almost immediately. Rush the food to your kitchen and your kettle as quickly as you can.

But even the most perfect food, prepared exactly, will spoil if not processed for the required time at the correct temperature.

Wash and sort fruits and vegetables, discarding any that are spoiled. Cut out bruises or blemishes. Unevenly shaped foods can go into jams and jellies; really ripe fruits and vegetables should be used immediately rather than canned. Sorting for uniform sizes and shapes, as well as ripeness, will help foods to cook more evenly. Jars of same-size shapes and pieces look prettier, too.

Washing fruits and vegetables before preparing is a necessity. Dirt harbors some of the dangerous bacteria, so scrub, wash, and rinse them well. At the same time, handle the fruits or vegetables carefully so you don't bruise any. Always lift foods out of washing or rinsing water and then let water and dirt drain off. Even if fruit is to be peeled, wash it first.

PLANNING

Decide now just how much of which foods you want to can. The total amount you can should be determined by the size of your family, what they like, and how much of those foods you will need until the next harvest. Available storage space will also affect the extent of your canning. Don't go overboard and can jars and jars of only one or two foods. Aim for an assortment—you'll appreciate having a variety of home-canned foods on hand.

Canning is becoming more and more popular and supplies can't always meet demand. Purchase jars and lids early in the season, so you'll have what you need come harvest time.

SCHEDULING

Organize your time when you plan to can. You will need several hours of relatively uninterrupted time to process fruits or vegetables from start to finish. Wise canners allow themselves a morning or two a week to put up several jars of just-right, just-ripe fruits and vegetables.

Never prepare more food than will fill a canner or kettle at one time. Thus the jar capacity of your processing container will determine how many jars you fill, how much food you prepare, and just how long each individual canning session will be.

You'll need to schedule kitchen space, as well as time. There must be room to set out all your canning equipment; space to wash, sort, and prepare food; and a sheltered spot for finished jars to cool. You'll also want to arrange for a minimum of traffic through the kitchen.

You'll be working with boiling water or steam under pressure, hot foods and containers, sharp knives, etc.—all potentially dangerous to little people.

CONTAINERS

Use *only* standard glass jars especially made for home canning. Ordinary glass jars and lids (peanut butter jars, for example) are not made to withstand the temperatures necessary for proper processing, and sealing is not complete with previously used noncanning jars.

Glass jars for canning come in three styles: regular mason jars, wide-mouth mason jars, and tapered jars suitable for canning or freezing. Pints and quarts are the usual sizes available. Closures may be two-piece self-sealing lids, with a flat metal lid and metal screw band, or the older-fashioned porcelain-lined zinc cap and rubber ring. The two-piece self-sealing closure is more

Two types of closures for glass canning jars.

common. Its flat metal lid may be used only once, but metal screw bands, if kept in good condition, can last through several canning seasons. Zinc caps use rubber rings as gaskets to seal at the shoulder of mason jars. These caps can be used over and over, but you must use new rubber rings each time. Don't test rings by stretching them.

Be sure to match lids to the size of the jar top. Always follow manufacturer's directions for each type of lid. *Read package directions before you start.* Follow manufacturer's directions for opening jars just as you do for closing them. After checking each jar for signs of spoilage (see "Safety Tips," page 42), open two-piece closures by puncturing the metal lid to break the seal, then carefully pry the lid up. To open jars sealed with a rubber ring and zinc cap, pull the jar rubber out (pliers help), then unscrew the cap.

Before starting any canning, check jars and lids for nicks, dents, scratches, cracks, sharp edges, or any other defects. Discard any damaged lids or jars.

Wash jars well in hot suds, and rinse them thoroughly in hot water. Keep jars in hot water until ready to use. Jars for jelly must be sterilized (see page 113), but jars to be processed in a boiling water bath or pressure canner need not be sterilized. Processing in boiling water or pressure canner will sterilize jars as food is processed.

Follow manufacturer's directions for any preparation of lids.

EQUIPMENT

In addition to a water bath canner (see A, page 20) or pressure canner (B), you'll also need:

several large kettles and pans (C)
vegetable brushes for scrubbing (D)
colander for draining (E)
food chopper for cutting or grinding (F)
1-quart measure (G)
long-handled tongs and forks to move food or
    jars (H)

Having the proper equipment is essential for successful canning. Shown here are some of the items described below. Line them up in advance so canning
day will go smoothly.

jar lifter to get hot jars in and out of water bath
   or pressure canner (I)
wide-mouthed funnel for filling jars (J)
narrow spatula or table knife to release air bubbles
   from jars (K)
folded cloth or wire rack to rest jars on as they
   are filled and as they cool (L)
a timer to keep track of processing (M)
cheesecloth for spice bags
pot holder or heat-proof mitt to protect hands
clean damp cloth to wipe rims and threads of jars
   after they are filled

STORAGE

Canned foods will keep for a year if they are stored in a
cool, dark, dry place. High temperatures, light, and
dampness can alter color and flavor and diminish quality. Freezing may not harm canned food, but jars or
seals could break or crack and food can then spoil. If
your storage spot is unheated, wrap jars in paper or
cover with a blanket to prevent freezing.

You'll notice that the step-by-step directions for boiling water bath and pressure canning tell you to wash
filled jars after cooling. Putting away sticky or dirty jars
could attract bugs or vermin.

PREPARATION METHODS

There are three preparation methods for foods before they are put in jars—open kettle, raw pack, and hot pack. Once the food is in the jars, for raw pack and hot pack it must be processed. Processing is done in a boiling water bath for fruits, tomatoes, pickles, jams, and preserves; processing is done in a pressure canner at 10 pounds pressure for all vegetables, meats, poultry, and fish.

Open kettle preparation means you cook food completely, then pack it while boiling hot into hot, sterilized jars, filling and sealing one jar at a time. Sterilized equipment—jars, tongs, spoons, ladles, funnels, anything you use—is a must! This method is used only for jams and jellies, preserves, conserves, butters, etc. The open kettle method is not recommended for any other foods and must *never* be used for meat or poultry. The possibilities for microorganism contamination are just too great.

Raw pack is just what the name implies. You pack uncooked fruits and vegetables, whole or in pieces, in clean, hot jars (no need to sterilize, because processing takes care of that). You then add boiling liquid—either water, syrup, juice, or cooking liquid—leaving some headspace for expansion during processing. Each recipe tells you exactly how much headspace for both solids and liquids. It's important to remove air bubbles from the jars by running a spatula or knife down the side of the jar. If the air bubbles are large, you may need to add more hot liquid to fill to within ½ inch of the top of the jar. Seal jars, following manufacturer's directions. Process in boiling water bath or pressure canner, as recipe directs. The processing both sterilizes and cooks the food.

Hot pack means that you cook the food before packing it into jars and processing. The cooked fruit or vegetable must be very hot as you put it into clean, hot jars (again, there is no need to sterilize jars, because processing takes care of that). You add hot cooking liquid, syrup, or boiling water, leaving proper headspace as the recipe directs. Remove air bubbles and add additional hot liquid, if needed. Then seal, following manufacturer's directions. Follow recipe directions for processing in boiling water bath or pressure canner.

PROCESSING

Every step in the preparation of foods for canning is important, but processing is the last and most important step.

Processing is heating prepared food in closed jars. It must be done at high enough temperatures and for enough time to destroy bacteria, yeasts, molds, and enzymes. There are two methods for processing canned foods: boiling water bath and pressure canner. The boiling water bath heats foods to 212°F. This is sufficient for pickles, relishes, fruits, and tomatoes. But vegetables, meat, poultry, and fish must be cooked to a higher temperature—240°F. This temperature is possible only as a result of steam under pressure, so you must use a pressure canner.

BOILING WATER BATH STEP BY STEP

You can buy a water bath canner in most department, houseware, or hardware stores, or you can put together your own from a large, deep kettle with a tight-fitting cover and a wooden or wire rack to stand on the bottom of the kettle. You might like to have a divider rack that sits in the kettle and holds jars both upright and away from each other. The kettle should be deep enough to allow 2 to 4 inches above the jars, as they sit on the rack, for rapidly boiling water. A deep pressure canner may be used for a boiling water bath, but leave the vent or petcock open and do not fasten the lid.

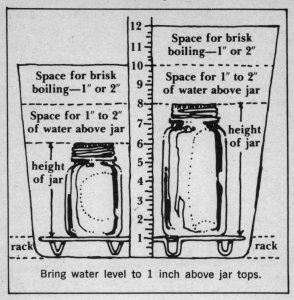

Bring water level to 1 inch above jar tops.

Follow these steps for processing canned foods in a boiling water bath:

1. Check jars and lids. Wash and rinse jars and keep hot. Follow manufacturer's directions to prepare lids.

Put water bath canner on range and pour in four to five inches of water. Turn heat on and, at the same time, start heating additional water in another large kettle or pot, so you'll have enough boiling water ready to cover jars in kettle by 1 inch.

2. Prepare food as recipe directs. Fill only enough jars to fill canner.

3. As each jar is filled, wipe rim and threads with clean, damp cloth. Seal, following manufacturer's directions. Place jar on rack in canner. Leave room between jars for boiling water to circulate.

4. Pour boiling water down sides of kettle, not directly onto jars, to bring water level to 1 inch above tops of jars.

BOILING WATER BATH

1. Pour 4 to 5 inches of water into water bath canner; heat to boiling.

2. Prepare food as recipe directs. Fill only enough jars to fill the canner.

step by step

3. Place each jar on rack in canner. Leave room between jars for boiling water to circulate.

4. Pour boiling water down sides of kettle, not directly onto jars, to bring water to 1 inch above jars.

Continued

5. Cover kettle and return to boiling as quickly as possible. Begin timing. Keep water boiling.

6. Process for times given in recipe. Check Altitude Chart; adjust time if you live above sea level.

7. After processing, turn heat off. Remove jars from canner to rack or folded cloth, away from drafts. Leave enough space between jars for air to circulate. Do not cover jars; do not put on cold or wet surface.

8. Let jars cool 12 to 24 hours. Test seal as manufacturer directs; remove screw bands.

9. Inspect jars for leakage or bubbles. If present, contents of jar must be used at once or reprocessed.

Continued

10. Wash jars in warm suds, rinse, dry, and label.

11. Store jars in a cool, dark, dry place. Before using, always check for signs of spoilage.

5. Cover kettle and return to boiling as quickly as possible. When water returns to boil, begin timing.

BOILING WATER BATH TIMETABLE

THIS METHOD OF PROCESSING IS RECOMMENDED FOR FRUITS, PICKLES, AND TOMATOES.

	MINUTES	
FRUITS	*Pints	Quarts
Apples	20	25
Applesauce	25	25
Apricots	20	25
Berries (except strawberries)	15	20
Cherries	20	20
Cranberries	10	10
Currants	20	20
Dried Fruits	15	15
Figs	30	30
Fruit Juices	10	10
Grapefruit	20	20
Grapes	20	20
Nectarines	20	25
Peaches	20	25
Pears	25	30
Pickles	See Pickle Timetable, page 70	
Pineapple	30	30
Plums	20	25
Rhubarb	10	10
Strawberries	15	15
Tomatoes	35	45
Tomatoes (Low Acid)	45	55
Tomato Juice	10	10
Tomatoes, Stewed	55	55

* The time in these tables for boiling water bath canning applies to half pint, pint, and quart jars.

ALTITUDE CHART

Increase processing time
if the time called for is:

ALTITUDE	20 MINUTES OR LESS	MORE THAN 20 MINUTES
1,000 feet	1 minute	2 minutes
2,000 feet	2 minutes	4 minutes
3,000 feet	3 minutes	6 minutes
4,000 feet	4 minutes	8 minutes
5,000 feet	5 minutes	10 minutes
6,000 feet	6 minutes	12 minutes
7,000 feet	7 minutes	14 minutes
8,000 feet	8 minutes	16 minutes
9,000 feet	9 minutes	18 minutes
10,000 feet	10 minutes	20 minutes

Water must boil continuously during processing time. Add boiling water, if necessary, to keep jars covered by 1 inch.

6. Process for time given in recipe. Times are for sea level. Check the Altitude Chart on this page, and adjust time accordingly if you live above sea level.

7. When processing time is finished, turn heat off. Remove jars from canner to rack or folded cloth, away from drafts. Leave enough space between jars for air to circulate. *Do not* cover jars and *do not* put them on a cold or wet surface. Follow manufacturer's directions for adjusting lids after processing.

8. After jars have cooled 12 to 24 hours, test seal as manufacturer directs and remove screw bands, if used. If band sticks, cover with hot, damp cloth for a minute, then try again. Don't store jars with band on.

9. Inspect jars for any leakage or bubbles. These signs mean contents of jar must be used at once or re-packed or reprocessed. If liquid has boiled out of a jar, do not open it to replace liquid but leave as is.

10. Wash jars well in warm suds, rinse, dry, and label.

11. Store jars in a cool, dark, dry place.

Before opening and using, always examine each jar for signs of spoilage. See "Safety Tips," page 42.

PRESSURE CANNING STEP BY STEP

A pressure canner should have a rack, a steamtight cover, a vent or petcock, a safety valve, and an accurate gauge or weight to measure pressure. You may use a pressure saucepan if it has a gauge that maintains 10 pounds of pressure and is large enough to accommodate pint jars.

Always read the instructions that come with your pressure canner or saucepan and follow them exactly. If your canner has a weight pressure control, be sure it is clean. It does not need to be tested because it has no moving parts to get out of order. If your canner has a dial pressure gauge, it should be checked for accuracy at the beginning of each canning season. Your county extension home economist will tell you how to do this. If you live at an altitude above 1000 feet check the chart on page 39 and adjust your pressure accordingly.

Always start with a clean canner. Wash, rinse, and dry canner and parts following manufacturer's instructions.

Follow these steps for processing foods in a pressure canner:

1. Check jars and lids. Wash and rinse jars and keep hot. Follow manufacturer's directions to prepare lids.

Prepare food as recipe directs.

2. When food is ready to be packed into jars, put pressure canner on range. Put rack in bottom and pour in 2 to 3 inches boiling water. Turn heat on.

3. As each jar is filled, wipe rim and threads with clean, damp cloth. Seal, following manufacturer's direc-

PRESSURE CANNING

1. Wash and rinse jars; keep hot. Prepare lids as manufacturer directs and food according to recipe.

2. Put pressure canner on range. Put rack in bottom; add 2 to 3 inches of boiling water and heat.

step by step

3. Fill each jar, wipe rim and threads with damp cloth. Seal and place jar on rack in canner.

4. Following manufacturer's directions, adjust pressure canner cover and fasten securely.

Continued

5. Exhaust canner with dial gauge by leaving vent or petcock open; let steam escape 7 to 10 minutes.

6. Process for time given in recipe. Adjust heat during processing to maintain even pressure.

7. After processing, remove canner from heat. Let canner stand till gauge registers zero. Open vent or petcock gradually. If no steam escapes, remove cover, tilting it away from you as you lift it.

8. Remove jars from canner to rack or folded cloth. Leave enough space between jars for air to circulate.

9. After jars have cooled, test seal as manufacturer directs. Remove screw bands before storing.

Continued

10. Inspect jars for any leakage or bubbles. Reprocess or use contents at once if present.

11. Wash jars, dry and label. Store in cool, dark, dry place. Check for signs of spoilage before using.

tions. Place jar on rack in canner. Leave room between jars for steam to circulate.

4. Following manufacturer's instructions, adjust pressure canner cover and fasten securely.

5. Exhaust canner with dial gauge by leaving vent or petcock open and letting steam escape freely for 7 to 10 minutes. Then close vent, or put on weighted gauge, following manufacturer's directions. When required pressure is reached, start timing. A weight control may be placed on the vent as soon as the cover is closed. Air is automatically exhausted from the canner when the control jiggles.

6. Process for time given in recipe. Adjust heat during processing to maintain even pressure. Times are for sea level. Check the Altitude Chart on page 39, and adjust pressure accordingly if you live above sea level.

7. When processing time is finished, remove canner from heat and turn heat off. Do not try to lower pressure, but let canner stand until gauge registers zero. Open vent or petcock gradually. If you see no steam escaping, pressure is down. If there is still some steam, let canner sit a little longer. To test for pressure with a weight control, nudge it. If no steam escapes, remove control. Remove cover, tilting it away from you as you lift so that steam comes out away from you.

8. Remove jars from canner to rack or folded cloth away from drafts. Leave enough space between jars for air to circulate. *Do not* cover jars and *do not* put on a cold or wet surface. Follow manufacturer's directions for adjusting lids after processing.

9. After jars have cooled for 12 to 24 hours, test seal as manufacturer directs and remove screw bands, if used. If band sticks, cover with hot damp cloth for a minute, then try again. Do not store jars with band on.

10. Inspect jars for any leakage or bubbles. These signs mean contents of jars must be used at once or repacked and reprocessed. If liquid has boiled out of a jar, do not open it to replace liquid but leave as it is.

11. Wash jars well in warm suds, rinse, dry, and label.

Store in a cool, dark, dry place.

Before opening and using, always examine each jar for signs of spoilage. See "Safety Tips," page 42.

PRESSURE CANNING TIMETABLE

ALL VEGETABLES, EXCEPT TOMATOES, CANNED AT HOME MUST BE HEATED TO BOILING, THEN COVERED AND BOILED 10 TO 15 MINUTES BEFORE TASTING OR USING.

	MINUTES		
VEGETABLES	Pints	Quarts	Pounds
Asparagus	25	30	10
Beans (green and wax)	20	25	10
Beans, lima	40	50	10
Beets	35	40	10
Carrots	25	30	10
Corn (cream style) pints only	95		10
Corn (whole kernel)	55	85	10
Eggplant	30	40	10
Greens (all kinds)	70	90	10
Hominy	60	70	10
Mushrooms	30		10
Okra	25	40	10
Onions	40	40	10
Peas (all shelled peas)	40	40	10
Peppers, bell	35		10
Peppers, pimento	10		5
Potatoes, Irish	40	40	10
Pumpkin	65	80	10
Rutabagas	35	35	10
Soybeans	80	80	10
Squash (summer)	30	40	10
Squash (winter)	65	80	10
Sweet potatoes (dry pack)	65	95	10
Sweet potatoes (wet pack)	55	90	10

ALTITUDE CHART
Pressure Canner (with dial gauge)

ALTITUDE	PROCESS AT:
2,000 – 3,000 feet	11½ pounds
3,000 – 4,000 feet	12 pounds
4,000 – 5,000 feet	12½ pounds
5,000 – 6,000 feet	13 pounds
6,000 – 7,000 feet	13½ pounds
7,000 – 8,000 feet	14 pounds
8,000 – 9,000 feet	14½ pounds
9,000 –10,000 feet	15 pounds

Note: If pressure canner has weighted gauge, above 2000 feet use 15 pounds pressure instead of 10.

TESTING FOR SEAL

When processed jars are cold, check them to be sure they are sealed. If the seal is not complete, empty the jar and use the food at once, or repack and reprocess. Here's how to test jars sealed with self-sealing flat metal lids (screw bands removed after processing).

Jars are sealed if:

1. When you press the center of the lid, it is already down and doesn't move.
2. When you tap center of the lid with a teaspoon it rings bright and clear.
3. When the jar is tipped or tilted slightly there is no leaking around the rim.

Jars sealed with rubber rings and porcelain-lined zinc caps are sealed if there is no leaking around the edge of cap when the jar is tipped or tilted slightly.

CANNING DO'S AND DON'TS

DO gather all equipment before you start to prepare food. Inspect all equipment to be sure it is in working order.

DO wash all equipment in hot suds and rinse well with hot water. Prepare lids as manufacturer directs. Keep jars hot until ready to fill.

DO follow established procedures and tested recipes. Short cuts and improper processing can have serious, even fatal, results.

DO avoid sudden changes in temperature which can break glass jars. Put hot food in hot jars and stand on rack or cloth-covered surface to cool.

DO keep a kettle of boiling water handy to add to water bath canner should the level go down and to fill jars of food to within ½ inch of top, if needed.

DO get a new dial gauge for your pressure canner if it is off by 5 pounds or more.

DO process same size jars of the same food in water bath or pressure canner.

DO label all jars with name of food, date, and any other pertinent information, such as no salt, honey-sweetened, etc.

DO wipe top and threads of each jar with a clean, damp cloth or paper towel before putting on lid.

DO remember that you're working with hot food, equipment, and containers. Reach for the pot holder before you reach for the jar!

DON'T try adding aspirin in place of heat processing, or attempt any other gimmicky preparation.

DON'T can in the oven. Jars can explode and temperatures are not high enough for safe processing.

DON'T use the open kettle method for anything but jams, jellies, butters, and similar preserves.

DON'T use canning powders or other chemical preservatives.

DON'T use any jars but those made for canning. Jars that you bought full of mayonnaise or peanut butter haven't been tempered to take the high temperatures of processing. Standard canning lids don't fit threads on these jars, anyway, so you can't get a perfect seal.

DON'T let foods stand in washing or cooking water any longer than absolutely necessary: they'll lose vitamins and flavor.

SAFETY TIPS

ALWAYS be on the lookout for spoilage.

BEFORE opening jars check for bulging or leaking.

AFTER opening jars check for spurting liquid, mold, bad smell, change in color, foaming, unusual softness, mushiness, or slipperyness.

IF YOU NOTICE ANY OF THESE SIGNS, DO NOT EAT OR EVEN TASTE. DISPOSE OF FOOD SO THAT NEITHER HUMANS NOR ANIMALS CAN EAT IT. (You can salvage the jar, however. Empty it, wash well and rinse, then boil the jar in clear water for 15 minutes.)

BRING HOME-CANNED VEGETABLES, MEAT, POULTRY, AND FISH TO BOIL, AND BOIL COVERED 10 TO 15 MINUTES BEFORE TASTING OR USING. Boil greens, corn, or other thick-massed foods 20 minutes and stir occasionally.

IF FOOD FOAMS OR DOESN'T SMELL RIGHT AFTER BOILING, DISPOSE OF FOOD SO THAT NEITHER HUMANS NOR ANIMALS CAN EAT IT.

WHEN IN DOUBT, THROW IT OUT!

DON'T raw pack vegetables if you live above 6000 feet. Use hot pack method only.

DON'T ever serve home-canned vegetables, meats, or poultry cold from the jar. See "Safety Tips," page 42.

WHAT WENT WRONG?

Here are answers to some common canning problems.

Cloudy liquid	May be a sign of spoilage, but more likely a result of minerals in hard water or starch in too-ripe vegetables. To be sure of quality, open food and boil, uncovered, 10 minutes. If food foams or smells bad, destroy it so that humans and animals can't eat it.
Colors changed	Darkening at top of jar may be from exposure to air in the jar or from underprocessing. Over-processing can discolor all the food in the jar, not just at the top. Minerals in hard water may cause some discoloration, too. These changes just listed are harmless, but color changes *can* indicate spoilage.
Bottom of metal lids discolored	This is due to natural compounds in foods corroding the lid. No need to worry: the discolored deposit is harmless.
Sediment in bottom of jars	A result of hard water or use of table salt instead of pickling salt. The food is all right to eat.

Jars lose some liquid during processing

Liquid can boil out if food has been packed into jars too tightly. Follow recipe directions carefully. Also be sure jars are completely covered with water all during processing or that pressure of pressure canner remains constant during processing. *Don't* open jars to add more liquid! They are all right as is.

Fruit floats in jar

Fruit was packed in too loosely, syrup used was too heavy, or some air may have remained in the fruit after heating and processing. See the recipe for strawberries on page 67 for no-float directions.

Jars did not seal

Probably a result of using non-standard jars; using lids or screw bands that have flaws; not following manufacturer's directions; or not wiping clean the sealing edge of jar after filling.

 # VEGETABLES

When canning vegetables at home, *all* vegetables *must* be processed in a pressure canner at 10 pounds pressure for the time given in the recipe. The importance of this rule for your health and safety can hardly be over-emphasized. We (and the USDA and all the other canning experts) urge you to follow it religiously. Tomatoes are a fruit, not a vegetable, but because they vary in acidity, either add bottled lemon juice or vinegar *or* process as for vegetables.

All vegetables canned at home MUST be heated to boiling, then covered and boiled 10 to 15 minutes BEFORE tasting or serving.

VEGETABLE CANNING TIPS

To precook vegetables, add just enough boiling water to cover them, then boil for the time given in the recipe. Keep vegetables boiling hot while packing them into jars.

Headspace is the amount of room you leave at the top of the jar. Each recipe tells you just how much space to leave between the top of the liquid and the top of the jar.

Get yourself a wide-mouth funnel for ease in filling jars.

Although recipes may call for the addition of salt, you do not have to add it. Salt supplies flavor only and is not necessary for preservation. If you do use salt, use only canning or pickling salt. Regular table salt can leave sediment at the bottom of jars and iodized salt can discolor foods.

Some cooks like to add 2 teaspoons of a sugar-salt mixture to each quart of corn, peas, beets, or tomatoes. For sugar-salt mixture, blend 2 parts sugar and 1 part salt.

Asparagus

Wash; trim off scales and tough ends and wash again. Measure length of jar, subtract ½ inch for headspace, and cut asparagus to that length, or cut into 1-inch pieces.

Raw pack: Pack in jars to within ½ inch of top. Add ½ teaspoon salt per pint. Fill with boiling water to within ½ inch of top of jar. Remove air bubbles. Add additional liquid, if needed, to fill to within ½ inch of top of jar. Seal, following manufacturer's directions.

Hot pack: Cook cut asparagus in boiling water 2 to 3 minutes. Pack in jars to within ½ inch of top. Add ½ teaspoon salt per pint. Fill with cooking water or boiling water to within ½ inch of top of jar. Remove air bubbles. Add additional liquid, if needed, to fill to within ½ inch of top of jar. Seal, following manufacturer's directions.

Tie bundles of jar-length asparagus and stand on end in 2 inches of boiling water. Cover and boil 3 minutes. Pack in jars, tips up. Add ½ teaspoon salt per pint. Fill with cooking water or boiling water to within ½ inch of top of jar. Remove air bubbles; add additional liquid, if necessary. Seal, following manufacturer's directions.

Process at 10 pounds pressure, 25 minutes for pints, 30 minutes for quarts.

Beans, Green or Wax

Wash beans, remove ends, and cut into even lengths.

Raw pack: Pack in jars to within ½ inch of top. Add

½ teaspoon salt per pint. Fill with boiling water to within ½ inch of top of jar. Remove air bubbles and add additional water, if needed, to fill to within ½ inch of top of jar. Seal, following manufacturer's directions.

Hot pack: Cover beans with boiling water, heat to boiling, and boil 3 minutes. Pack in jar to within ½ inch of top. Add ½ teaspoon salt per pint. Fill with cooking water or boiling water to within ½ inch of top of jar. Remove air bubbles and add additional water, if needed, to fill to within ½ inch of top of jar. Seal, following manufacturer's directions.

Process at 10 pounds pressure, 20 minutes for pints, 25 minutes for quarts.

Cover beans with boiling water; boil 2 to 3 minutes. Pack loosely in jars; add cooking water.

Beans, Lima

Select young, tender beans. Wash, shell, and wash again.

Raw pack: Pack loosely in jars to within 1 inch of top. Add ½ teaspoon salt per pint. Fill with boiling water to within ½ inch of top of jar. Remove air bubbles and add additional liquid, if necessary, to fill to within ½ inch of top. Seal, following manufacturer's directions.

Hot pack: Cover beans with boiling water, heat to boiling, and boil 2 to 3 minutes. Pack loosely in jars to within 1 inch of top. Add ½ teaspoon salt per pint. Fill with cooking water or boiling liquid to within ½ inch of top of jar. Remove air bubbles; add additional liquid, if needed, to fill to within ½ inch of top. Seal, following manufacturer's directions.

Process at 10 pounds pressure, 40 minutes for pints, 50 minutes for quarts.

Beans, Soy

Use green soy beans and follow recipe for Lima Beans.

Process at 10 pounds pressure, 55 minutes for pints, 65 minutes for quarts.

Beets

Select small, uniform beets. Cut off tops, leaving about 1 to 2 inches of stem. Cook in boiling water about 15 to 25 minutes or until skins slip off easily. Remove skins, tops, and roots. Pack in jars to within ½ inch of top. Add ½ teaspoon salt or 1 teaspoon sugar-salt mixture per pint. Fill with boiling water to within ½ inch of top of jar. Remove air bubbles and add additional water, if needed, to fill to within ½ inch of top. Seal, following manufacturer's directions.

Process at 10 pounds pressure, 35 minutes for pints, 40 minutes for quarts.

Carrots

Wash and peel carrots; wash again. Slice or dice, or leave whole if young and tender.

Raw pack: Pack in jars to within ½ inch of top. Add ½ teaspoon salt per pint. Fill with boiling water to within ½ inch of top of jar. Remove air bubbles. Add additional water, if needed, to fill to within ½ inch of top of jar. Seal, following manufacturer's directions.

Hot pack: Cover carrots with boiling water, heat to boiling, and boil 2 to 3 minutes. Pack in jars to within ½ inch of top. Add ½ teaspoon salt per pint. Fill with cooking water or boiling water to within ½ inch of top of jar. Remove air bubbles and add additional liquid, if needed, to fill to within ½ inch of top. Seal, following manufacturer's directions.

Process at 10 pounds pressure, 25 minutes for pints, 30 minutes for quarts.

Corn, Whole Kernel

Select tender, juicy corn, just fresh from the field, if possible. Remove husks and silk. Cut off any damaged spots. Wash ears using a brush. Cut corn from the cob at about ⅔ the depth of the kernel.

Raw pack: Pack loosely in jars to within 1 inch of top. Add ½ teaspoon salt or 1 teaspoon sugar-salt mixture per pint. Fill with boiling water to within ½ inch of top of jar. Remove air bubbles and add additional liquid, if needed, to fill to within ½ inch of top. Seal, following manufacturer's directions.

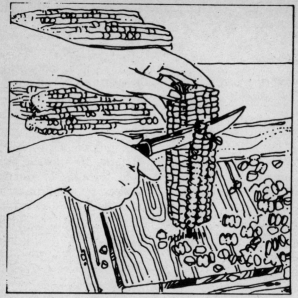

Cut corn at about ⅔ the depth of the kernel.

Hot pack: Cover corn with boiling water, heat to boiling, and hold at boiling temperature while packing loosely in jars to within 1 inch of top. Add ½ teaspoon salt or 1 teaspoon sugar-salt mixture per pint. Fill with cooking liquid or boiling water to within ½ inch of top of jar. Remove air bubbles and add additional liquid, if needed, to fill to within ½ inch of top. Seal, following manufacturer's directions.

Process at 10 pounds pressure, 55 minutes for pints, 85 minutes for quarts.

Corn, Cream Style

Select fresh, tender, juicy corn, and hurry it from field to kitchen. Remove husks and silk. Cut off any damaged spots. Wash ears using a brush. Cut corn from cob at about the center of the kernel, then scrape cobs with the back or dull edge of the knife to get the cream. Use pint jars only.

Raw pack: Pack corn in pint jars to within 1½ inches of top. Add ½ teaspoon salt to each jar. Fill with boiling water to within ½ inch of top of jar. Remove air bubbles; add additional liquid, if needed, to fill to within ½ inch of top. Seal, following manufacturer's directions.

Hot pack: Add just enough boiling water to cover corn; heat to boiling and boil 3 minutes. Pack loosely in jars to within 1 inch of top. Add ½ teaspoon salt to each jar. Fill with cooking liquid or boiling water to within ½ inch of top. Remove air bubbles and add additional liquid, if needed, to fill to within ½ inch of top of jar. Seal, following manufacturer's directions.

Process at 10 pounds pressure, 95 minutes.

Peas (all shelled varieties)

Use only young, tender, and very fresh peas. Wash, shell, and wash again.

Raw pack: Pack loosely in jars to within 1½ inches of top. Add ½ teaspoon salt or 1 teaspoon sugar-salt mixture per pint. Fill with boiling water to within ½ inch of top of jar. Remove air bubbles and add additional liquid, if needed, to fill to within ½ inch of top. Seal, following manufacturer's directions.

Hot pack: Cover with boiling water; heat to boiling and boil 2 minutes. Pack loosely in jars to within 1 inch of top. Add ½ teaspoon salt or 1 teaspoon sugar-salt mixture per pint. Fill with cooking water or boiling water to within ½ inch of top. Remove air bubbles and add additional liquid, if needed, to fill to within ½ inch of top of jars. Seal, following manufacturer's directions.

Process at 10 pounds pressure, 40 minutes for pints and quarts.

Pumpkin

Cut pumpkin in medium pieces and pare. Steam until tender, about 25 minutes. Put pumpkin and any cooking water through food mill, sieve, or blender. Add spices, if desired. Simmer strained pumpkin until hot, stirring often to prevent sticking. Pack loosely in jars to within ½ inch of top. Remove air bubbles but add no liquid or salt. Seal, following manufacturer's directions.

Process at 10 pounds pressure, 65 minutes for pints, 80 minutes for quarts.

Spinach and all other greens

Select freshly picked, tender leaves. Remove tough stems and bruised or blemished leaves. Wash thoroughly in several waters, always lifting spinach out of water each time. Cook spinach, covered, with only the water that clings to the leaves, just until wilted. Cut through greens several times with sharp knife or kitchen shears. Pack loosely in jars to within 1 inch of top. Add ½ teaspoon salt per pint. Fill with boiling water to within ½ inch of top. Remove air bubbles; add additional liquid, if needed, to fill to within ½ inch of top of jars. Seal, following manufacturer's directions.

Process at 10 pounds pressure, 70 minutes for pints, 90 minutes for quarts.

Squash, Summer and Zucchini

Wash well but do not peel. Slice, halve, or quarter into evenly sized pieces.

Raw pack: Pack in jars to within 1 inch of top. Add ½ teaspoon salt per pint. Fill with boiling water to within ½ inch of top of jar. Seal, following manufacturer's directions.

Hot pack: Cover with boiling water and heat until boiling resumes. Pack in jars to within 1 inch of top. Add ½ teaspoon salt per pint. Fill with cooking or boiling water to within ½ inch of top of jar. Remove air bubbles and add additional liquid, if needed, to fill to within ½ inch of top of jar. Seal, following manufacturer's directions.

Process at 10 pounds pressure, 30 minutes for pints, 40 minutes for quarts.

Squash, Winter

Follow directions for pumpkin.

Tomatoes

Although tomatoes are fruits, they are used most often as vegetables and so they are included here.

Select firm, ripe, unblemished tomatoes. Wash; then scald in boiling water 15 seconds, just long enough to loosen peels. Plunge into cold water, then drain. Peel, core, and quarter. (Note: Because tomatoes vary in acidity, either add 2 tablespoons bottled lemon juice or vinegar to each quart *or* process at 10 pounds pressure for 5 minutes.)

Raw pack: Pack firmly in jars to within ½ inch of top. Add no liquid, but push down so tomatoes are covered with their own juice. Add ½ teaspoon salt or 1 teaspoon sugar-salt mixture per pint. Seal, following manufacturer's directions.

Process in boiling water bath, 35 minutes for pints, 45 minutes for quarts.

Hot pack: Heat tomatoes to boiling. Pack in jars to within ½ inch of top. Add ½ teaspoon salt or 1 teaspoon sugar-salt mixture per pint. Remove air bubbles. Seal, following manufacturer's directions.

CANNING TOMATOES

1. Check manufacturer's instructions for filling and sealing jars. Set out all equipment needed.

2. Check jars for nicks, cracks, or sharp edges. Use new lids. Heat water in half-filled water bath canner.

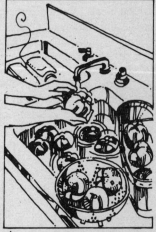

3. Wash and rinse jars and caps. Leave jars in hot water until ready to use.

4. Use firm, red-ripe tomatoes. Don't can any with decayed spots or cracks. Wash only enough tomatoes for one canner load.

step by step

5. Put tomatoes in wire basket or cheesecloth in boiling water about ½ minute to loosen skins. Dip into cold water. Drain.

6. Cut out all cores, remove skins, and trim off any green spots. Cut tomatoes in quarters or leave whole.

7. Pack tomatoes in hot jar. Press tomatoes until spaces fill with juice. Leave ½-inch headspace.

8. Add a teaspoon salt per quart. Run knife between tomatoes and jar to release air bubbles.

9. Wipe top of jar with damp cloth. Put red rubber sealing compound of lid next to jar. Screw band on tight.

10. As each jar is filled, stand it on rack in canner of hot, not boiling water. Water should cover jars 1 to 2 inches.

11. Cover canner. Bring to a boil. At altitudes less than 1000 feet above sea level, process pints 35 minutes, quarts 45 minutes at a gentle boil.

12. Remove jars. Let cool for 12 hours. Remove bands. Test for seal by pressing center of lid. If dome stays down, jar is sealed.

Process in boiling water bath, 10 minutes for pints and quarts.

Tomato Juice

Select firm, ripe tomatoes. Wash, scald, peel, and cut into chunks. Simmer until soft, stirring occasionally to prevent sticking. Put through sieve or food mill. Add ½ teaspoon salt per pint and heat to boiling. Pour immediately into hot jars to within ½ inch of top. Seal, following manufacturer's directions.

Process in boiling water bath, 10 minutes for pints and quarts.

(Top) Scald tomatoes for easy peeling. (Lower right) Pack firmly in jars; push down so tomatoes are covered with their own juice.

Vegetables, Mixed

Select any combination of vegetables you like. Prepare each vegetable as recipe directs. Mix together and boil 3 minutes. Pack as directed for those vegetables that you use. Process for time of vegetable that requires longest processing time.

ALWAYS HEAT HOME-CANNED VEGETABLES, MEAT, POULTRY, AND FISH TO BOILING. COVER AND BOIL 10 TO 15 MINUTES BEFORE TASTING OR USING.

 # FRUITS

Fruits must be processed in a boiling water bath for the time indicated in the recipes that follow or in the Boiling Water Bath Timetable on page 29.

Fruits should be packed in jars to within ½ inch of the top of the jar. To raw pack, fill the jar of fruit with hot syrup, fruit juice, or water to within 1½ inches of top of jar. To hot pack, fill the jar of fruit with hot syrup, fruit juice, or water to within ½ inch of top of jar. Remember to remove air bubbles by running a spatula or knife down the side of the jar. If air bubbles are large, you may need to add more hot liquid, to bring it up to within either ½ inch or 1½ inches of top of jar.

DARKENING AND DISCOLORATION

To prevent darkening and discoloration of canned fruits, as you prepare the fruit, drop it into salted water (1½ teaspoons salt per quart of cold water); drain when ready to pack or cook. Adding ascorbic acid or vitamin C tablets to each jar will also help prevent discoloration during processing. You can use a commercial ascorbic acid and citric acid color-keeping mixture, following manufacturer's directions, or add five tablets (50 milligrams each) to each quart jar before putting the fruit in. Or you may add ½ teaspoon crystalline ascorbic acid to each quart of syrup before you pour it over the fruit in the jars.

SWEETENING

Most recipes for canning fruits call for sweetening to be added in the form of sugar syrup (see "Syrup How-To," page 62), but honey, corn syrup, or low-calorie artificial sweeteners may also be used. If fruit is very juicy you can skip the syrup and heat to simmering each quart of raw prepared fruit with ½ cup sugar. Use the resulting liquid to pour over the fruit in the jars.

Calorie-conscious cooks often pack fruits in fruit juice or just plain water. If you use an artificial sweetener, check and follow the manufacturer's directions.

Use honey or light corn syrup for no more than one half the amount of the sugar called for in the recipe. Any more than one half the amount will overpower the fruit flavors—honey-flavored fruit then becomes fruit-flavored honey. Brown sugar, molasses, sorghum, or other strongly flavored syrups are not used in canning for the same reason—they overpower the fruit flavor and darken fruits, too.

SYRUP HOW-TO

To make a syrup for packing and sweetening canned fruits, combine sugar and water in the amounts given in the chart and boil until the sugar dissolves. Use fruit juice in place of water, if you wish. Once the sugar is dissolved, reduce heat. Keep syrup hot, but do not allow it to boil or it will evaporate and thicken.

Apples

Select uniform apples. Wash, pare, core, and cut into quarters, slices, or halves. Keep pared fruit in salt water while preparing. Drain. Boil 5 minutes in only enough thin syrup or water to cover. Pack in clean, hot jars to within ½ inch of top. Fill with hot syrup or water to within ½ inch of top. Remove air bubbles; add additional hot syrup or water, if necessary, to fill to within ½ inch of top of jar. Seal, following manufacturer's directions.

Process in boiling water bath, 20 minutes for pints, 25 minutes for quarts.

Applesauce

Select 20 large apples. Wash, quarter, core, and remove all bruised or decayed parts. Keep cut fruit in salt water while preparing. Drain. Add 1 quart water and cook until tender. Press through sieve or colander to remove peel. Stir in 2½ cups sugar (more or less, according to tartness of apples and your taste) and heat to boiling. Pack in clean, hot jars to within ½ inch of top. Seal, following manufacturer's directions. Makes about 4 pints.

Process in boiling water bath, 25 minutes for pints and quarts.

Apricots

Follow directions for peaches. Peel, or don't peel, as you wish.

Berries (all except cranberries and strawberries)

Wash and sort berries. Use imperfect berries to heat with water and sugar for syrup.

Raw pack: Pack berries in clean, hot jars to within ½ inch of top. Fill with hot light or medium syrup to within 1½ inches of top of jar. Remove air bubbles; add additional hot syrup, if needed, to fill to within 1½ inches of top of jar. Seal, following manufacturer's directions.

Hot pack (for firm berries): Heat berries to boiling in medium or heavy syrup. Pack in clean, hot jars and fill with hot syrup to within ½ inch of top of jar. Remove air bubbles; add additional hot syrup, if needed, to fill to within ½ inch of top of jar. Seal, following manufacturer's directions.

Process in boiling water bath, 15 minutes for pints, 20 minutes for quarts.

SYRUP HOW-TO

Type of Syrup	For	Cups Sugar +	Cups Water or Juice =	Cups Syrup
Thin	small, soft fruits	2	4	5
Medium	peaches, apples, pears sour berries	3	4	5½
Heavy	sour fruits or extra sweetness	4¾	4	6½

Note: A 1-quart jar of fruit needs 1 to 1½ cups syrup.

Cherries

Wash, stem, and pit cherries.

Raw pack: Pack in clean, hot jars and shake down to within ½ inch of top. Pour hot medium or heavy syrup (depending on sweetness of cherries) to within 1½ inches of top. Remove air bubbles; add additional hot syrup, if needed, to fill to within 1½ inches of top of jar. Seal, following manufacturer's directions.

Process in boiling water bath, 20 minutes for pints and quarts.

Cranberries

Wash and pick over berries. Remove stems. Add to boiling heavy syrup and boil 3 minutes. Pack into hot, *sterilized* jars to within ½ inch of top. Fill with hot syrup to within ½ inch of top. Remove air bubbles.

Add additional syrup, if needed, to fill to within ½ inch of top of jar. Seal, following manufacturer's directions.

Process in boiling water bath, 10 minutes for pints and quarts.

Cranberry Sauce

Wash and pick over 1 quart berries. Add 1 cup water and cook until soft. Press through sieve or food mill. Add sugar and boil 3 minutes. Pour into hot, *sterilized* pint jars to within ½ inch of top. Seal, following manufacturer's directions. Makes about 2 pints.

Process in boiling water bath, 10 minutes for pints.

Currants

Follow recipe for berries.

Process in boiling water bath, 20 minutes for pints and quarts.

Fruit, Mixed

Use any combination of fruit you like, excluding bananas and oranges. Wash, peel, if necessary, and cut fruit to desired size. Pack in clean, hot jars. Fill to within 1½ inches of top with hot medium syrup. Remove air bubbles; add additional liquid, if needed, to fill to within 1½ inches of top. Seal, following manufacturer's directions.

Process in boiling water bath for time of fruit requiring the longest processing.

Grapes

Wash grapes and remove stems. Pack tightly into clean, hot jars, without crushing, to within ½ inch of top. Fill with medium syrup to within 1½ inches of top of jar. Remove air bubbles and add additional syrup, if necessary, to fill to within 1½ inches of top of jar. Seal, following manufacturer's directions.

Process in boiling water bath, 20 minutes for pints and quarts.

Peaches

Select firm, ripe fruit. Drop into boiling water just a minute or two, until skins slip; then plunge into cold water and drain. Peel, halve, and pit. Keep peeled and cut fruit in salt water while preparing the rest. Drain.

Raw pack: Pack halves, cut side down, or slices into clean, hot jars to within ½ inch of top. Fill with hot medium syrup to within 1½ inches of top of jar. Remove air bubbles. Add additional liquid, if needed, to fill to within 1½ inches of top of jar. Seal, following manufacturer's directions.

Hot pack: Heat fruit to boiling in medium syrup; boil 3 to 5 minutes. Add 1 teaspoon lemon juice to each quart, if desired. Pack into clean, hot jars to within ½ inch of top. Fill with hot cooking syrup to within ½ inch of top. Remove air bubbles and add additional syrup, if needed, to fill to within ½ inch of top. Seal, following manufacturer's directions.

Process in boiling water bath, 20 minutes for pints, 25 minutes for quarts.

Pears

Wash, pare, halve, and core fruit. Keep pared fruit in salt water while preparing the rest. Drain.

Raw pack (for ripe, soft fruit): Pack in jars to within ½ inch of top. Fill with hot medium syrup to within 1½ inches of top. Remove air bubbles; add additional syrup, if needed, to fill to within 1½ inches of top. Seal, following manufacturer's directions.

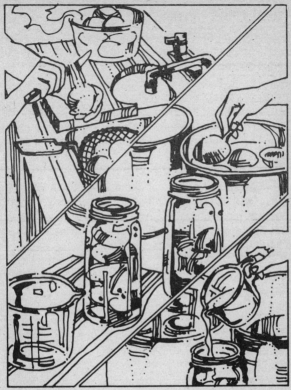

(Top) Peaches can be peeled easily if they are dipped in boiling water, then in cold. (Middle) Pack halves or slices in jars to ½ inch of top. (Bottom) Cover with boiling syrup leaving ½-inch space at top of jar.

Hot pack: Heat fruit to boiling in thin or medium syrup; boil 5 to 6 minutes. Pack into clean, hot jars to within ½ inch of top. Fill with hot cooking syrup to within ½ inch of top. Remove air bubbles; add additional syrup, if needed, to fill to within ½ inch of top of jar.

Process in boiling water bath, 25 minutes for pints, 30 minutes for quarts.

Plums

Select firm plums that are not too ripe. Wash well, then prick each plum several times with a needle to prevent bursting.

Raw pack: Pack firmly in jars. Fill with hot medium syrup to within 1½ inches of top of jar. Remove air bubbles. Add additional syrup, if needed, to fill to within 1½ inches of top. Seal, following manufacturer's directions.

Hot pack: Heat plums to boiling in medium or heavy syrup. Pack in jars and fill with hot cooking syrup to within ½ inch of top. Remove air bubbles. Add additional liquid, if needed, to fill to within ½ inch of top of jar. Seal, following manufacturer's directions.

Process in boiling water bath, 20 minutes for pints, 25 minutes for quarts.

Rhubarb

Wash and cut in ½- to 1-inch pieces.

Raw pack: Pack tightly in clean, hot jars to within ½ inch of top. Fill with hot light or medium syrup to within 1½ inches of top. Remove air bubbles. Add additional syrup, if needed, to fill to within 1½ inches of top. Seal, following manufacturer's directions.

Hot pack: Sprinkle rhubarb with ¼ cup sugar for each quart of cut fruit and let stand several hours to draw out juice. Heat to boiling and pack in clean, hot jars to within ½ inch of top of jar. Seal, following manufacturer's directions.

Process in boiling water bath, 20 minutes for pints, 25 minutes for quarts.

Strawberries

Select firm, ripe, red strawberries. Strawberries will fade and lose color when canned, but the following method of preparation will prevent them from floating in the jar.

Hull, rinse, drain, and measure 6 cups of berries, cutting large berries in half. Take out about ½ to 1 cup of the softer berries. Crush them and heat to make ½ cup juice. Heat the juice and 2 cups sugar to boiling; cool and add the whole strawberries. Heat to boiling and boil 3 minutes. Cover and set aside for 4 hours. Pack in clean, hot jars to within ½ inch of top. Seal, following manufacturer's directions.

Process in boiling water bath, 15 minutes for pints and quarts.

PICKLES AND RELISHES

Pickles add crispness, tang, and flavor to almost any meal or snack, and no pickles taste better than those you've made yourself! Our pickle section includes recipes for the four general types of pickles: brined, fresh pack, fruit pickles, and relishes, as well as recipes for chutneys, catsup, and chili sauce. Put up some of each for your family to enjoy. Pack a few extra jars for holiday, shower, housewarming, or anytime gifts.

WHO'S WHO IN THE PICKLE FAMILY

Brined or fermented pickles must be cured or fermented in brine (salt water) for about 3 weeks. Dill pickles, sauerkraut, and green tomatoes usually get this long-term treatment. Cukes become olive or yellow green on the outside, translucent on the inside. Good brined pickles have a tender, firm skin that is not hard, rubbery, or shriveled. They are tender, but firm to the bite. Kraut should have a pleasant tart and tangy flavor with no off-flavor or odor. Kraut to be proud of is crisp and firm and a bright creamy-white.

Fresh-pack or quick-process pickles include cross-cut slices, bread and butter pickles, and dilled green beans. They get a brief brine treatment of several hours or overnight; then they are mixed with boiling vinegar and spices. Soft olive green is the preferred color for this group of pickles. They should be crisp and tender, yet firm.

Relishes include an assortment of fruit and vegetables that are chopped, seasoned, and cooked. Chutneys, piccalilli, horseradish, and corn relish belong to this group.

Flavors of relishes may be mild and sweet, or pungent and hot. Cut vegetables and fruit in uniform pieces for pretty-looking jars.

Fruit pickles are whole or cut fruits cooked in a spicy sweet and sour syrup. Tender but firm, brightly colored, and evenly sized pieces are the bywords for beautiful fruit pickles.

Catsup and sauces can be made from fruits or vegetables that are highly spiced, then boiled down to a thick liquid. Catsup is usually strained, sauce isn't.

FOODS FOR PICKLING

Pick the best to make the best. Pickling can capture the flavor and tenderness of perfect fruits and vegetables, but it can't be any help to foods that are too ripe, too green or otherwise not quite right.

Old-time cooks used to add alum and lime to crisp and firm pickles, but if you select good, fresh produce and follow the recipes exactly you won't need to bother with these additives.

Fruits and vegetables *must* be *fresh*. If you can't prepare and process them just as soon as they've been picked or purchased, refrigerate them at once. Cucumbers especially start to lose freshness the minute they come off the vine.

Discard any moldy produce. Don't use waxed cucumbers for pickling whole—the brine can't get through the wax to the cucumber. Choose a variety of cucumber that's grown especially for pickling.

Vegetables should be young and tender, fruits firm but ripe. Slightly underripe peaches and pears are fine for pickling.

PICKLE TIMETABLE

PICKLES AND RELISHES		MINUTES
Bread and Butter	qt.	10
Bread and Butter	pt.	5
Chutney	pt.	5
Cross Cut Slices	pt.	5
Dill Green Beans	pt.	5
Gherkins, Sweet	pt.	5
Piccalilli	pt.	5
Pepper-Onion Relish	pt.	5
Relish, Corn	pt.	15
Watermelon	pt.	5

FRUIT PICKLES

Peaches	qt. or pt.	20
Pears	qt. or pt.	20

Start counting processing time as soon as water returns to boil.

PICKLES—DILL

Fermented (whole)	qt.	15
Unfermented (whole)	qt.	20
(Fresh pack dills)		

SAUERKRAUT qt. 15

Start counting processing time as soon as filled jars are placed in actively *boiling* water.

PREPARATION

Pick over fruits and vegetables and select those of the same size to prepare and process. Uniformity of sizes means more even cooking, even doneness, ease in handling and packing, and prettier jars.

Scrub vegetables and thoroughly wash fruits, handling gently to avoid bruising. Always lift fruits and vegetables out of wash water. If you leave them in water and let it drain off, dirt gets deposited right back on the food.

Remove all blossoms from cucumbers.

PROCESSING

All pickles and relishes must be processed in a boiling water bath to prevent spoilage. Each recipe gives the processing time. You may cherish some older recipes that call for pickles to be prepared by the open kettle method, but there is danger of spoilage microorganisms getting in the food as it goes from kettle to jar, no matter how clean and careful you are, so do process pickles in a boiling water bath.

STORAGE

Store pickles just as you do other canned foods—in a cool, dark, dry place. Some of the recipes that follow are for refrigerator pickles. Store as those recipes direct.

INGREDIENTS

Salt, vinegar, sugar, water, and spices are the ingredients for pickles, and each one of them plays an important part in the pickling process.

Pure granulated pickling or canning salt is a must for pickling. Table salt has substances added to keep it from caking and these substances can cloud the brine. Iodized salt can darken pickles. Too much salt can ruin pickles, just as can too much of any other ingredient, and excess salt can toughen and shrivel vegetables, so follow directions carefully.

Vinegar should be of good quality, clear, and with no sediment. Some prefer the flavor of cider vinegar, while others use white (distilled) vinegar to help preserve the natural color of light-colored fruits and vegetables. Always use vinegar that is 4 percent to 6 percent acid—the label will tell you. A vinegar solution that is too strong can bleach and/or soften fruits and vegetables,

BRINED DILL PICKLES

1. Wash cucumbers thoroughly with a brush. Use several changes of cold water. Take care to remove all blossoms. Drain on rack.

2. Place half of the spices and a layer of dill on the bottom of a 5-gallon jar or crock. Fill with cucumbers to within 3 or 4 inches of top. Cover with remaining dill and add rest of spices. Mix salt, vinegar, and water, and pour over cucumbers.

3. Cover cucumbers with heavy plate or glass lid, with weight to keep the cucumbers under the brine. A jar filled with water makes a good weight.

4. Bubbles and the formation of scum indicate active fermentation. Scum should be removed daily.

73

Continued

5. After 3 weeks of fermentation, the dills are ready for processing. Cloudiness of the brine results from yeast development during fermentation. Strain the brine before using.

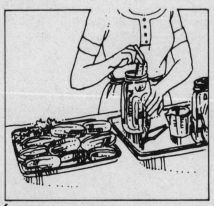

6. Pack pickles firmly into clean, hot quart jars. Don't wedge tightly. Add several pieces of dill to each jar. Cover with boiling brine to within ½ inch of jar top; adjust lids. Process in boiling water for 15 minutes. Start timing as soon as hot jars are placed in the actively boiling water.

7. Remove jars from the canner and complete seals if necessary. Set jars up-right, several inches apart, on a wire rack to cool. Cloudiness of brine is typical when the original fermentation brine is used as the covering liquid.

while a too-weak solution can soften and/or spoil the food you've worked so hard to put away. Never dilute vinegar unless the recipe specifically directs you to do so. If you want a finished product that is less sour, add sugar rather than decreasing vinegar.

Granulated white sugar is preferred for pickling. If the recipe calls for brown sugar, use it, but otherwise don't substitute.

Water is water, you may say—but not necessarily. Hard water can interfere with the fermenting of pickles, so use soft water to make brine. If you don't have soft water, boil hard water, let it stand 24 hours and then remove the scum. Strain water through several thicknesses of cheesecloth to remove the sediment. Some cooks recommend adding a tablespoon of vinegar per gallon of boiled water before using, to further reduce hardness.

WHAT WENT WRONG?

Here are the likely causes of some common problems in making pickles.

Shriveled   Too much vinegar, sugar, or salt, or too much cooking or processing.

Hollow   Too rapid fermentation, brine too strong or too weak for proper fermentation, or cucumbers were poorly developed or not fresh.

Soft or slippery   Usually caused by spoilage as a result of too little acid or salt, not enough brine or heat treatment, poor seal on jars, scum in brine during fermentation, moldy garlic or spices, or blossoms left on cucumbers. *Do not use*.

Dark   Use of ground spices or too much spice, use of iodized rather than pickling salt, use of hard water or iron utensils, or overcooking.

Spices should be fresh and preferably whole, since whole spices give better and longer-lasting flavor than ground spices. Tie the whole spices loosely in a cheesecloth spice bag. To make a spice bag, cut a double thickness of cheesecloth about 5 inches square. Put whole spices in the center and tie the corners firmly together. Remove spice bag before packing pickles into jar.

CONTAINERS

Just as for all other home canning of foods, standard glass canning jars are the recommended containers for pickles and relishes. Check jars and lids for defects and discard those that are not flawless. Wash and rinse jars before use and keep them hot. Prepare lids as manufacturer directs. Jars do not need to be sterilized since the boiling water bath processing does that.

EQUIPMENT

The highly acid and salt nature of pickles requires special selection of utensils for fermenting and preparing. Unchipped enamel, aluminum, stainless steel, and glass kettles and utensils are best for cooking the pickle liquid or pickles themselves. Do not use copper, brass, galvanized, or iron utensils, because they can discolor or chemically react with pickles. A crock or stone jar, unchipped enamel-lined pan, or large glass jar, bowl or casserole is best for fermenting or brining. Use a large heavy plate or glass lid which fits *inside* the brining container, and place a weight or jar full of water on the cover to hold the vegetables under the brine. A large heavy-duty plastic food bag partly filled with water can take the place of a lid and weight.

The utensils listed on pages 19-20 are those you will need for pickling. In addition, it's nice to have a scale for greater accuracy in measuring ingredients. The correct proportion of cabbage to salt for sauerkraut is better based on weight than measure.

PICKLING STEP BY STEP

1. Gather all equipment and all ingredients. Check jars and lids. Wash and rinse all equipment. Keep jars hot. Follow manufacturer's directions to prepare lids.

2. Put water bath canner on range and pour in 4 to 5 inches of water. Turn heat on and at the same time start heating additional water in another large kettle or pot, so you will have enough boiling water ready to cover the jars in the kettle by 1 inch.

3. Wash food thoroughly and prepare as recipe directs. Fill only enough jars to fill canner.

4. Pack jars firmly, but not so tightly that brine or

syrup can't get around and over food. Leave headspace as recipe directs. Remove air bubbles by working a narrow spatula or table knife carefully up and down sides of jar. Add extra syrup or brine as the recipe directs to bring liquid back up to 1½ inches from the top for raw pack, ½ inch for hot pack. Wipe the rim and threads of the jar with a clean damp cloth or paper towel.

5. Seal jars as manufacturer directs. Put jars on rack in canner in boiling water, leaving room between the jars for boiling water to circulate.

6. Add boiling water, if necessary, to keep jars covered by 1 inch. Do not pour boiling water directly on the jars.

7. Cover the kettle and bring water back to boiling as rapidly as possible. When boiling resumes, start timing for the number of minutes given in each recipe, except for dill pickles. Timing for dill pickles begins as soon as the jars go into the boiling water bath. (See Pickle Timetable, page 70.)

8. Process in the boiling water bath for the time given in the recipe. Times are for sea level. Check the Altitude Chart for boiling water bath on page 30 and adjust time accordingly if you live above sea level.

9. When processing time is finished, turn heat off. Remove jars from canner immediately to rack or folded cloth on a dry surface, away from drafts. Leave enough space between the jars for air to circulate. *Do not* cover jars and *do not* put them on cold or wet surface. Follow manufacturer's directions for adjusting lids after processing.

10. Let jars cool 12 to 24 hours. When jars are cold, test seal as manufacturer directs and remove screw bands, if used. If bands stick, cover with a hot damp cloth for a minute, then try again. Don't store jars with bands on.

11. Inspect jars for any leakage or bubbles. These signs mean the contents of the jar must be used at once or repacked and reprocessed. If liquid has boiled out of a jar, do not open it to replace liquid. Leave as is.

12. Wash jars in warm suds, rinse, dry, and label.

13. Store jars in a cool, dark, dry place.

14. Before opening and using, always examine jars for signs of spoilage. See "Safety Tips" on page 42. If pickles are soft or slippery, do not use.

Brined Dill Pickles

20 pounds (about ½ bushel) 3- to 6-inch cucumbers
¾ cup whole mixed pickling spice
2 to 3 bunches fresh or dried dill
2½ cups vinegar
1¾ cups pure granulated salt
2½ gallons water

1. Wash cucumbers thoroughly in cold water, scrubbing with vegetable brush. Handle carefully to avoid bruising. Drain or wipe dry.

2. In 5-gallon crock or jar, arrange half the pickling spice and a layer of dill. Fill with cucumbers to within 3 or 4 inches of top. Sprinkle with remaining pickling spice and top with another layer of dill.

3. Combine remaining ingredients and pour over. Cover with plate or lid that fits inside crock or with plastic bag filled with water. Weight plate or lid to help it hold cucumbers under brine (a jar of water works fine). Cover loosely with a clean cloth. Set aside at room temperature.

4. Remove scum daily and discard. (It may take 3 to 5 days for scum to form.) Do not stir pickles. Be sure pickles are completely covered with brine. Add additional brine, if necessary, to keep them covered, using 3 tablespoons salt per quart of water.

5. Let pickles ferment about 3 weeks, or until olive green in color and well flavored. Brine will be cloudy, due to yeast having developed during fermentation. New brine can be made to use for processing, but it will not be as flavorful as the fermentation brine. (For new brine use ½ cup salt, 4 cups vinegar, and 1 gallon water.)

6. Pack pickles, along with some dill, into clean, hot jars. Add a clove of garlic to each jar, if desired. Do not pack too tightly.

7. Strain brine and heat to boiling. Fill jars with brine to within ½ inch of top of jar. Seal, following manufacturer's directions.

8. Process in boiling water bath for 15 minutes. Start counting processing time as soon as jars go into the boiling water, rather than from the time the water returns to a boil.

9 to 10 quarts pickles

Sliced Cucumber Pickles

6 pounds cucumbers (about 4 inches long), thinly
    sliced (do not pare)
4 large onions, shredded (about 1 quart)
2 green peppers, shredded (about 2 cups)
½ cup salt
  Small ice cubes
5 cups cider vinegar
5 cups sugar
1½ teaspoons ground turmeric
2 tablespoons mustard seed
2 tablespoons plus 2 teaspoons celery seed
16 whole cloves

1. Mix the vegetables and salt in a large bowl or earthenware crock. Cover with ice cubes and top with a weighted plate; set aside about 3 hours. Drain.

2. Meanwhile, blend vinegar and remaining ingredients together in a large kettle. Add drained vegetables. Heat

thoroughly over medium heat (do not boil), stirring occasionally with a wooden spoon.

3. Pack in clean, hot jars to within ½ inch of top. Fill with hot syrup to within ½ inch of top of jar. Remove air bubbles.

4. Seal, following manufacturer's directions.

5. Process in boiling water bath 10 minutes.

8 pints pickles

Bread and Butter Pickles
(Midwestern Style)

> 2 quarts ¼-inch cucumber slices (about 16
>   cucumbers, 4 to 5 inches each)
> ½ cup coarse salt
> 1 quart boiling water
> 2 cups chopped onion
> 2 cups chopped green pepper
> ¾ cup chopped red pepper
> 2 cups cider vinegar
> 2 cups sugar
> 1 teaspoon celery seed
> 1 teaspoon mustard seed
> ¾ teaspoon ground turmeric

1. Prepare the cucumber slices and toss with salt in a large bowl. Pour boiling water over cucumbers, cover, and let stand overnight.

2. The next day prepare the chopped vegetables.

3. Combine remaining ingredients in a large saucepot and stir over medium heat until sugar is dissolved. Increase heat and bring to boiling. Add the chopped vegetables and cucumbers and cook gently about 5 minutes.

4. Immediately pack the pickles to within ½ inch of top of clean, hot jars. Remove air bubbles. Seal, following manufacturer's directions.

5. Process in boiling water bath 5 minutes.

About 4 pints pickles

1. Remove outer leaves from firm, mature cabbage heads; wash and drain. Remove core or cut it into thin shreds.

2. Shred cabbage and weigh 5 pounds. Weight must be accurate to insure the correct proportion of cabbage to salt.

3. Measure 3 tablespoons pure granulated salt and sprinkle over 5 pounds of shredded cabbage.

step by step

4. Allow the salted cabbage to stand a few minutes to wilt slightly. Mix well, with clean hands or a spoon, to distribute salt uniformly.

5. Pack the salted cabbage into container. Press firmly with wooden spoon, tamper, or with hands until the juices drawn out will just cover the shredded cabbage.

Continued

6. Place a water-filled plastic bag on top of the cabbage. This will fit snugly against the sides of the container and prevent exposure to air. After fermentation, remove bag of water. Transfer sauerkraut to kettle to simmer.

7. Pack hot sauerkraut into clean, hot jars; add juice to within ½ inch of jar tops. Adjust lids. Process jars in boiling water bath; 15 minutes for pints, 20 minutes for quarts. Start timing as soon as jars are placed in boiling water.

8. Remove jars from the canner and complete seals if necessary. Set jars upright, several inches apart, on a wire rack to cool.

Sauerkraut

About 50 pounds firm, mature, green cabbage
1 pound (1½ cups) pure granulated salt

1. Remove outer leaves and any blemishes or bad parts of cabbage; wash and drain. Cut each head in halves, then quarters, and remove core.
2. Using knife or shredder, cut cabbage in shreds the thickness of a dime.
3. Weigh 5 pounds of shredded cabbage. In large container mix this cabbage with 3 tablespoons salt. Let stand several minutes or until slightly wilted.
4. Pack wilted cabbage firmly and evenly into large clean crock or jar. Use wooden spoon or tamper or clean hands and press cabbage down firmly until juice comes to surface.
5. Repeat wilting and packing (in same large contain-

WHAT WENT WRONG?

Did your sauerkraut not turn out right? Here are answers to some common problems.

Soft kraut   Too little salt, too high a temperature during fermentation, uneven distribution of salt, or air pockets from poor packing.

Pink kraut   Too much salt, uneven distribution of salt, or poor covering or weighting of kraut during fermentation, which causes certain types of yeast to flourish in kraut.

Rotten kraut Not covered tightly, allowing air to get to surface of kraut.

Dark kraut   Unwashed and poorly trimmed cabbage; not enough juice to cover fermenting cabbage; uneven distribution of salt; exposure to air; kept too warm during fermentation, processing and storage; or too long storage.

---

er) with 5 pounds shredded cabbage and 3 tablespoons salt until container is filled to within 3 to 4 inches of top.

6. Arrange a large, heavy-duty plastic food bag on top of the cabbage. (Use two bags for extra protection if you wish.) Fill the bag with water until you have added enough water to cover the surface of the cabbage and the weight of the water is enough to hold the cabbage down. The water bag should fit snugly against the sides of the container, to completely cover and seal the cabbage.

7. Let sauerkraut ferment at room temperature about 5 to 6 weeks. The gas bubbles you see are proof that the kraut is fermenting.

8. When fermentation has stopped, remove plastic bag. Heat sauerkraut to simmering (185° to 210°F) but *do not boil*. Pack into clean, hot jars. Fill with hot sauerkraut juice to within ½ inch of top of jar.

9. Seal, following manufacturer's directions.

10. Process in boiling water bath 15 minutes for pints, 20 minutes for quarts. Start timing as soon as jars are placed in boiling water.

16 to 18 quarts sauerkraut

Yellow Cucumber Pickles
(Senfgurken)

    12 large, ripe cucumbers
    ½ cup coarse salt
    4½ cups water
    1 quart cider vinegar
    6 cups sugar
    2 tablespoons yellow mustard seed
    1 tablespoon whole cloves
    1 piece (3 inches) stick cinnamon

1. Wash, pare, and halve the cucumbers lengthwise; remove seeds. Cut each half through center, crosswise, then cut each quarter into lengthwise pieces of desired thickness. Let stand 12 hours, or overnight, in a brine made of the salt and water. Drain cucumbers thoroughly.

2. Bring vinegar, sugar, and spices, tied in a spice bag, to boiling in a large kettle; add cucumbers. Cook gently until pieces begin to look transparent but are still crisp.

3. Pack in clean, hot jars to within ½ inch of top. Fill with hot syrup to within ½ inch of top of jar. Remove air bubbles.

4. Seal, following manufacturer's directions.

5. Process in boiling water bath 5 minutes.

About 3 quarts pickles

Crispy Icicle Pickles

>   4 pounds firm medium cucumbers
>   1 quart cider vinegar
>   ½ cup sugar
>   ½ cup salt
>   1 tablespoon mustard seed
>   1 tablespoon celery seed

1. Wash cucumbers, but do not peel. Cut into length-wise quarters or eighths and soak in ice water 5 hours. Add ice as necessary to keep water cold. Drain and pack in clean, hot jars.
2. Combine vinegar, sugar, salt, mustard seed, and celery seed in a saucepan. Bring to boiling; boil 1 minute.
3. Fill jars with hot liquid to within ½ inch of top. Remove air bubbles and add more hot liquid, if needed, to fill jars to within ½ inch of top.
4. Seal, following manufacturer's directions.
5. Process in boiling water bath 15 minutes.

6 pints pickles

Note: Let stand for 4 to 6 weeks before using.

Crispy Pickle Chunks

Follow recipe for Crispy Icicle Pickles; cut cucumbers into crosswise pieces.

Green Tomato Pickles

      8 pounds green tomatoes, thinly sliced
      6 large onions, thinly sliced
         Salt
      2 tablespoons whole cloves
      2 tablespoons whole allspice
      2 tablespoons mustard seed
      2 teaspoons mixed pickling spices
   3½ cups cider vinegar
      2 cups sugar
      2 teaspoons dry mustard
      2 large red peppers, coarsely chopped

1. Put tomatoes and onions into separate bowls; sprinkle tomatoes with ¼ cup salt and onions with 2 tablespoons salt. Cover and let stand 12 hours.
2. Drain vegetables thoroughly; discard liquid.
3. Tie whole spices in a spice bag and put into a large kettle; add vinegar and a mixture of the sugar and dry mustard. Heat to boiling, stirring until sugar is dissolved.
4. Add tomatoes, onions, and red peppers; cook slowly, uncovered, until tomatoes are just tender, about 20 minutes.
5. Pack in clean, hot jars. Fill with vinegar mixture to within ½ inch of top. Remove air bubbles. Add more vinegar mixture, if needed, to fill jars to within ½ inch of top.
6. Seal, following manufacturer's directions.
7. Process in boiling water bath 5 minutes.

4 pints pickles

Pickled Carrots

   3 pounds young carrots
      Boiling salted water
   2 teaspoons whole cloves
   2 teaspoons whole allspice
   1 teaspoon whole mace
   1 piece (3 inches) stick cinnamon
   3 cups white vinegar
   ½ cup water
   2 cups sugar

1. Cook washed carrots in boiling salted water until skins slip easily (carrots are only partially cooked). Drain and remove skins. If carrots are very small, leave whole; if large, cut lengthwise into halves or quarters.

2. Tie spices loosely in spice bag and put into a saucepan with remaining ingredients. Bring to boiling and boil gently 10 minutes.

3. Pour the hot syrup over carrots in a saucepan; set aside several hours.

4. Place over medium heat and bring to boiling; cover and boil gently 5 minutes. Remove spices.

5. Pack carrots in clean, hot jars to within ½ inch of top. Fill with boiling syrup to within ½ inch of top. Remove air bubbles. Add more syrup, if needed, to fill jars to within ½ inch of top. Seal, following manufacturer's directions.

6. Process in boiling water bath 10 minutes.

3 pints pickled carrots

Dill Pickles, Kosher Style

    4 pounds cucumbers (4 inches each)
    3 cups cider vinegar
    3 cups water
    6 tablespoons pure granulated salt
    14 cloves garlic, halved
       Dill seed
       Peppercorns

1. Scrub cucumbers and halve lengthwise.
2. Mix vinegar, water, salt, and garlic in a saucepan; bring to boiling.
3. Pack cucumbers in clean, hot 1-pint jars. Add 2 tablespoons dill seed, 3 peppercorns, and 4 garlic halves (from the pickling liquid) to each jar.
4. Fill jars with hot pickling liquid to within ½ inch of top of jar. Remove air bubbles and add more liquid, if needed, to fill jar to within ½ inch of top.
5. Process in boiling water bath 20 minutes. Start timing as soon as jars are put into boiling water bath.

7 pints pickles

Mustard Pickles

(Chowchow)

    1 large head cauliflower, rinsed and separated in
       flowerets (about 1½ quarts)
    1 quart small white pickling onions, peeled
    1 quart gherkin or small cucumbers, scrubbed
    1 quart small green tomatoes, washed and
       blossom ends removed
    2 large green peppers, cleaned and chopped
       (about 2 cups)
    2 large sweet red peppers, cleaned and chopped
       (about 2 cups)
    ½ cup salt
    3 quarts cold water

2 quarts cider vinegar
6 tablespoons prepared mustard
1½ cups packed light brown sugar
⅔ cup all-purpose flour
2 tablespoons ground turmeric

1. Prepare the vegetables and combine in a large bowl. Cover with a salt solution made by dissolving salt in cold water. Cover and set aside 24 hours.
2. Drain the salt solution from vegetables through a colander into a saucepan. Bring solution to boiling and immediately pour over vegetables in the colander. Set aside to drain.
3. Meanwhile, in a large heavy saucepan, combine the vinegar, mustard, and a mixture of the brown sugar, flour, and turmeric; blend thoroughly. Cook and stir with a wooden spoon over medium heat until thickened and smooth.
4. Add the drained vegetables and cook gently until they are tender but not soft. Stir frequently to prevent scorching. (Mixture is quite thick.)
5. Working quickly, pack pickles in clean, hot jars to within ½ inch of top. Remove air bubbles.
6. Seal, following manufacturer's directions.
7. Process in boiling water bath 10 minutes.

11 pints pickles

Pickled Onions

Boiling water
2 quarts small white onions
½ cup salt
1 quart white vinegar
1 cup sugar
2 tablespoons mixed pickling spices

1. Pour boiling water over onions; let stand 2 minutes. Drain and cover with cold water.

2. Peel onions and put into a bowl or crock. Add enough cold water to cover, sprinkle with the salt, and set aside overnight.

3. The following day, drain onions; rinse with cold water and drain thoroughly.

4. Mix white vinegar and sugar in a saucepan; add spices, tied in a spice bag, and bring to boiling.

5. Remove from heat and remove spice bag; pack onions in clean, hot jars. Fill with hot syrup to within ½ inch of top of jar. Remove air bubbles and add more syrup, if needed, to fill jars to within ½ inch of top.

6. Seal, following manufacturer's directions.

7. Process in boiling water bath 5 minutes.

About 5 pints pickled onions

Delicious Red Pepper Pickles

    12 large sweet red peppers (about 3½ pounds)
    2½ cups cider vinegar
    1¼ cups sugar
     1 piece (3 inches) stick cinnamon
    12 whole cloves

1. Wash peppers, quarter lengthwise, remove seeds and white membrane, and cut quarters into ¾-inch strips.

2. Pour boiling water over peppers in a bowl; cover and set aside about 3 minutes. Drain off the water and immediately cover peppers with icy cold water. Set aside about 10 minutes.

3. Meanwhile, combine vinegar with the remaining ingredients (cloves tied in cheesecloth) in a saucepan; bring to boiling, stirring until sugar is dissolved. Boil 2 to 3 minutes.

4. Drain peppers in a colander, reserving liquid. Pack in clean, hot jars. Fill with hot vinegar mixture to within ½ inch of top of jar. Remove air bubbles and add more liquid, if needed, to fill jars to within ½ inch of top.

5. Seal, following manufacturer's directions.
6. Process in boiling water bath 10 minutes.

3 pints pickles

Ginger Pickled Beets

    10 to 15 cooked beets
    3 cups vinegar
    1 cup water
    2 tablespoons prepared horseradish
    2 tablespoons sugar
    1 teaspoon ground mace
    1 teaspoon ground ginger
    ½ teaspoon ground cloves

1. If beets are small, leave whole; if large, slice. Put beets into a clean, hot quart jar or 2 pint jars.
2. Combine vinegar, water, horseradish, sugar, and spices in a saucepan. Bring to boiling; boil 2 minutes.
3. Fill jars with hot liquid to within ½ inch of top. Remove air bubbles and add more hot liquid, if needed, to fill jars to within ½ inch of top.
4. Seal, following manufacturer's directions.
5. Process in boiling water bath 15 minutes.

1 quart pickled beets

Note: Let stand 24 hours before serving.

Zucchini Pickle Slices

    2½ pounds zucchini, scrubbed, rinsed, and cut in
        ¼-inch slices (2½ cups)
    ¾ pound onions, thinly sliced (2½ cups)
    2 cups cider vinegar
    1 cup sugar
    4 to 5 tablespoons salt
    1½ teaspoons celery seed
    ¼ to ½ teaspoon ground turmeric

1. Prepare vegetables and set aside.
2. Mix remaining ingredients in a heavy saucepan. Cook and stir over medium heat until sugar is dissolved and mixture comes to boiling. Remove from heat. Immediately add the vegetables; cover and let stand about 1 hour.
3. Bring the vegetable mixture to boiling rapidly; reduce heat and cook gently, uncovered, about 3 minutes. Remove from heat.
4. Pack vegetables in clean, hot jars; add hot pickling liquid to within ½ inch of top, being sure that vegetables are completely covered. Remove air bubbles and add more syrup, if needed, to fill jars to within ½ inch of top.
5. Seal, following manufacturer's directions.
6. Process in boiling water bath 15 minutes.

About 4 pints pickles

Pickled Green Beans

    2 pounds fresh green beans
    2 quarts water
    ¾ cup cider vinegar
    ½ cup coarse salt
    1 teaspoon whole peppercorns
    1½ teaspoons mixed pickling spices
    ¼ cup dill seed
    2 bay leaves

1. Wash beans and break off ends. Cook beans in **boiling salted water** 8 minutes. Drain and pack into clean hot jars.
2. Combine water, vinegar, coarse salt, peppercorns, pickling spices, dill seed, and bay leaves in a large deep saucepan. Bring to a full rolling boil.
3. Fill jars with hot vinegar mixture to within ½ inch of top. Remove air bubbles and add more hot mixture, if needed, to fill jars to within ½ inch of top.
4. Seal, following manufacturer's directions.

5. Process in boiling water bath 15 minutes.

2 quarts pickles

Note: Let stand at least 2 days for flavors to penetrate beans.

Spiced Lemon Pickles

      9 large lemons
   2¼ cups sugar
     ⅛ teaspoon salt
      1 cup cider vinegar
     ¼ cup water
      1 stick cinnamon
     ½ teaspoon whole allspice
      1 piece ginger root
      4 whole cloves

1. Wash and dry lemons. Cut, without peeling, into ¼ inch thick crosswise slices (about 6 cups).
2. Combine sugar, salt, vinegar, and water in a saucepan. Tie cinnamon, allspice, ginger, and cloves in cheesecloth and add to saucepan. Bring to boiling; boil 5 minutes. Remove spice bag. Drop lemon slices into syrup; boil 1 minute.
3. Pack slices into clean, hot jars. Fill jars with hot syrup to within ½ inch of top. Remove air bubbles and add more hot syrup, if needed, to fill jars to within ½ inch of top.
4. Seal, following manufacturer's directions.
5. Process in boiling water bath 15 minutes.

6 half-pints pickles

Spiced Cantaloupe

2 very firm, underripe cantaloupes
1 cup cider vinegar
1 cup water
½ pound brown sugar (about 1⅓ cups packed)
½ cup sugar
10 whole cloves
1 piece (3 inches) stick cinnamon, broken in
    small pieces
½ teaspoon whole mace

1. Remove rind and seeds and cut cantaloupe into 1-inch cubes. (There should be about 2 quarts cubes.)
2. Put cubes into a bowl; cover with a salt solution of 2 tablespoons salt dissolved in 1 quart icy cold water. Invert a plate over fruit to keep cubes submerged in solution. Set aside 2 hours, then drain thoroughly.
3. Combine the vinegar, water, sugars, and the spices in a large heavy saucepan. Bring to boiling and add the drained melon. Cook, uncovered, over medium heat until cubes are almost transparent, stirring occasionally.
4. Using a slotted spoon, pack cantaloupe in clean, hot jars. Fill with hot syrup to within ½ inch of top. Remove air bubbles and add more syrup, if needed, to fill jars to within ½ inch of top.
5. Seal, following manufacturer's directions.
6. Process in boiling water bath 15 minutes.

3 pints pickles

Sweet Dilled Pear Pickles

6 pounds fresh Bartlett pears
2 cups sugar
1 cup vinegar
1 cup water
2 teaspoons whole allspice
2 teaspoons whole cloves
5 fresh dill heads

1. Combine **1 gallon cold water** and **2 tablespoons** each **salt and vinegar** in a bowl.

2. Halve, pare, and core pears. Cut into quarters or sixths, depending on size desired. Drop into water in bowl to prevent pears from darkening while preparing remaining pears and the syrup.

3. Combine sugar, vinegar, and water in a large kettle. Tie allspice and cloves in cheesecloth and add to kettle. Bring to boiling, stirring until sugar is dissolved. Cover; simmer 10 minutes.

4. Drain and rinse pears in cold water. Add to syrup and return to boiling. Cook 3 minutes.

5. Spoon pears carefully into clean, hot jars. Add a dill head to each jar. Fill jar with hot syrup to within ½ inch of top. Remove air bubbles and add more syrup, if needed, to fill to within ½ inch of top.

6. Seal, following manufacturer's directions.

7. Process in boiling water bath 20 minutes.

5 pints pickles

Curry Pears

    3¾ pounds small fresh Bartlett pears
    ¾ cup sugar
    ⅔ cup water
    ½ cup vinegar
    1 teaspoon curry powder
    3 slices lemon

1. Combine **1 gallon cold water** and **2 tablespoons** each **salt and vinegar** in a bowl.

2. Halve, pare, and core pears; drop into water in bowl as they are prepared to prevent pears from darkening.

3. Combine sugar, water, vinegar, and curry powder in a kettle; bring to boiling, stirring until sugar is dissolved.

4. Drain and rinse pears in cold water. Add to syrup and bring to boiling. Cover and cook about 8 minutes, or until just tender.

5. Pack pears carefully into clean, hot jars, adding a lemon slice to each. Fill jars with hot syrup to within

½ inch of top. Remove air bubbles and add more syrup, if needed, to fill to within ½ inch of top.

6. Seal, following manufacturer's directions.

7. Process in boiling water bath 20 minutes.

3 pints preserved fruit

Spiced Fresh Peaches

25 firm ripe peaches (about 6 pounds)
Whole cloves
2 cups sugar
2 cups cider vinegar
3 pieces (3 inches each) stick cinnamon
1 teaspoon whole allspice
2½ cups packed light brown sugar

1. Rinse and plunge peaches into boiling water to loosen skins. Plunge into cold water and gently slip off skins.

2. Insert 2 or 3 cloves into each peach and put into large kettle. Cover with boiling water and cook 5 minutes, or until almost tender. Drain, reserving ½ cup liquid for syrup.

3. Mix sugar, reserved peach liquid, vinegar, and cinnamon in a 4-quart kettle. Tie allspice in a spice bag and add to mixture. Boil 5 minutes.

4. Add one layer of peaches at a time to syrup, lower heat and simmer until peaches are thoroughly heated, 2 to 3 minutes. Remove to a large bowl. Repeat until all peaches have been heated.

5. Remove spice bag from syrup and pour syrup over peaches. Cover and let stand overnight.

6. The next morning, drain syrup from peaches into a 4-quart kettle; add brown sugar and bring to boiling, stirring until sugar is dissolved. Add peaches and bring syrup to full rolling boil. Remove from heat.

7. Pack hot peaches in clean, hot jars. Fill with hot syrup to within ½ inch of top of jar. Remove air bubbles and add more syrup, if needed, to fill jars to within ½ inch of top.

8. Seal, following manufacturer's directions.
9. Process in boiling water bath 20 minutes.

3 quarts spiced peaches

Note: Allowing peaches to stand in syrup overnight prevents shriveling and floating.

Watermelon Pickles

    2 pounds prepared watermelon rind
    ½ cup salt
    2 quarts water
    1 teaspoon whole allspice
    1 teaspoon whole cloves
    ¼ teaspoon mustard seed
    5 pieces (2 inches each) stick cinnamon
    3 cups vinegar
    2 cups water
    2 pounds sugar
    Green or red food coloring (optional)

1. Pare the watermelon rind, removing all green and pink portions. Cut the rind into 2 × 1 × ½-inch pieces.
2. Prepare a brine of the salt and 2 quarts water; pour over rind. Cover and let stand overnight.
3. Drain rind; cover with fresh water and cook until tender when pierced with a fork. Remove from heat and let stand several hours; drain.
4. Tie the spices loosely in a spice bag or cheesecloth. Put into a large saucepot with the remaining ingredients. Bring to boiling and cook 5 minutes. Add the drained watermelon rind and cook gently until rind is

clear and transparent. If desired, several minutes before end of cooking time, add enough green or red food coloring to the syrup to delicately tint the pickles. Remove and discard the spice bag.

5. Pack pickles in clean, hot jars. Fill with hot syrup to within ½ inch of top of jar. Remove air bubbles and add more syrup, if needed, to fill jars to within ½ inch of top.

6. Seal, following manufacturer's directions.

7. Process in boiling water bath 10 minutes.

About 3 pints pickles

Pickled Crab Apples

2½ pounds firm crab apples with stems
1½ tablespoons whole cloves
2 pieces (3 inches each) stick cinnamon
1½ tablespoons whole allspice
3 cups vinegar
6 cups sugar
3 cups water

1. Wash crab apples and remove the blossom ends. Do not peel. Run a large needle through crab apples to keep them from bursting during cooking.

2. Tie the spices loosely in a cheesecloth bag.

3. Combine vinegar, sugar, and water in a kettle; add the spices and bring mixture to boiling; boil 5 minutes.

4. Add crab apples, a layer at a time, and cook gently until tender, about 10 minutes.

5. Using a slotted spoon, remove crab apples to a large bowl or crock. Repeat until all crab apples are cooked.

6. Pour the boiling syrup over crab apples; cover and let stand in a cool place 12 to 18 hours.

7. Using a slotted spoon, remove crab apples from syrup and pack in clean, hot jars; remove spice bag from syrup.

8. Heat the syrup to boiling and quickly pour over crab apples. Remove air bubbles and add more syrup,

if needed, to fill jars to within ½ inch of top. Seal, following manufacturer's directions.

9. Process in boiling water bath 15 minutes.

About 4 pints pickles

Pear and Tomato Chutney

    4 pounds fresh Bartlett pears
    1 pound tomatoes
    2 cups chopped onion
    1 tablespoon minced garlic
    1 cup sugar
    1 cup vinegar
    1 teaspoon ground ginger
    1 teaspoon dry mustard
    1 teaspoon salt
    ¼ teaspoon cayenne pepper
    ½ cup chopped green pepper
    ½ cup chopped sweet red pepper

1. Pare, core, and dice pears to measure about 8½ cups. Skin tomatoes; remove and discard cores. Finely chop enough tomato to measure 2 cups.

2. Combine pears, tomatoes, onion, garlic, sugar, vinegar, ginger, mustard, salt, and cayenne in a kettle. Bring to boiling, stirring occasionally. Simmer, uncovered, 25 to 30 minutes, until pears are transparent and liquid is thickened. Add green and red pepper; cook 5 minutes. Ladle into clean hot jars, filling to within ½ inch of top.

3. Seal, following manufacturer's directions.

4. Process in boiling water bath 5 minutes.

4 pints chutney

Brandied Mincemeat

1 pound lean beef, cut in 2-inch cubes
5 pounds tart apples
½ pound suet
½ pound seedless raisins, chopped
1 pound currants
¼ pound candied citron, chopped
¼ pound candied orange peel, chopped
2 tablespoons grated orange peel
1 tablespoon grated lemon peel
¼ cup orange juice
2 tablespoons lemon juice
2 cups sugar
1 teaspoon salt
½ teaspoon pepper
1 teaspoon ground cinnamon
½ teaspoon ground cloves
½ teaspoon powdered coriander seed
½ teaspoon ground mace
½ teaspoon ground nutmeg
2 cups apple cider
1 can (16 ounces) tart red cherries with juice
½ pound walnuts, coarsely chopped
1 cup brandy

1. Put beef cubes into a small heavy saucepan with ½ to 1 cup boiling water; cover tightly and cook slowly until almost tender, about 1 hour. (Water should all be absorbed.) Cool.
2. Meanwhile, wash, quarter, core, and pare the apples; coarsely chop or put though coarse blade of a food chopper to yield about 6 cups chopped apples.
3. Finely chop the cooled meat and suet, or put through coarse blade of food chopper. Combine in a heavy saucepot with all the ingredients except walnuts and brandy.
4. Cook slowly, uncovered, for 2 hours or until thickened, stirring frequently to prevent sticking.

5. Stir in the walnuts and cook several minutes longer; add the brandy and blend well.

6. Remove from heat and quickly ladle the mincemeat into clean, hot jars. Seal, following manufacturer's directions.

7. Process in pressure canner at 10 pounds pressure for 25 minutes.

About 7 pints mincemeat

Note: A double-crust pie requires about 4 cups (2 pints) of mincemeat.

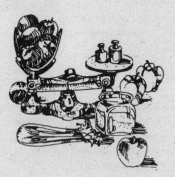

Chili Sauce

    5 pounds ripe tomatoes, peeled (about 15 medium)
    4 medium green peppers, membrane and
        seeds removed
    4 medium onions, peeled
    2 stalks celery
 1⅓ cups cider vinegar
 1⅓ cups sugar
    4 teaspoons salt
 ½ teaspoon black pepper
 ½ teaspoon ground cloves
 ¼ teaspoon ground cinnamon

1. Finely chop the vegetables or put through coarse blade of food chopper; combine in a large saucepot with the vinegar and a mixture of the remaining ingredients.

2. Bring to boiling and cook slowly, uncovered, 1½ to

2 hours, or until sauce is of desired thickness. Stir occasionally.

3. Ladle immediately into clean, hot jars. Seal, following manufacturer's directions.

4. Process in boiling water bath 5 minutes.

About 4 pints chili sauce

Green Tomato Mincemeat

  24 to 28 medium green tomatoes, finely chopped
       (about 4 quarts)
   8 to 10 medium tart apples, pared, cored, and
       finely chopped (about 2 quarts)
   1 pound raisins
   ¼ cup finely chopped candied citron, lemon,
       or orange peel
   2 cups water
   2 teaspoons salt
   1 tablespoon ground cinnamon
   ¼ teaspoon ground allspice
   ¼ teaspoon ground cloves
   5 cups packed brown sugar
   1 cup cider vinegar

1. Combine all ingredients and cook slowly until tomatoes are tender and mixture is slightly thickened; stir frequently to prevent sticking.

2. Fill clean, hot jars to within ½ inch of top.

3. Seal, following manufacturer's directions.

4. Process in boiling water bath 10 minutes.

About 6 pints mincemeat

Note: If desired, substitute 2½ cups granulated sugar for 2½ cups brown sugar; reduce vinegar to ¾ cup and add ¼ cup lemon juice.

Mango Chutney

1¼ cups sugar
1 cup cider vinegar
1 teaspoon chili powder
1 large clove garlic, minced
2 tablespoons finely chopped preserved ginger
4 cups sliced ripe mangos (two 1-pound mangos)
½ cup seedless raisins
½ cup sliced blanched almonds
½ teaspoon salt

1. Heat sugar and vinegar in a large saucepan to dissolve sugar; boil 5 minutes. Add chili powder, garlic, and ginger. Cook 5 minutes, stirring occasionally.
2. Mix in mangos and cook until mixture is transparent. Stir in raisins, almonds, and salt; cook until thickened.
3. Fill clean, hot jars to within ½ inch of top.
4. Seal, following manufacturer's directions.
5. Process in boiling water bath 5 minutes.

6 half-pints chutney

Aunt Vinnie's Piccalilli

1 quart chopped cabbage
1 quart chopped green tomatoes (about 8 medium)
1 cup chopped green pepper
½ cup chopped sweet red pepper
1 cup chopped onion
3 cups cider vinegar
1¾ cups sugar
1 tablespoon dry mustard
1½ teaspoons ground ginger
¼ teaspoon ground cinnamon
¼ teaspoon ground cloves
¼ teaspoon ground mace
1 tablespoon mustard seed
¼ teaspoon dried hot red pepper

1. Prepare the vegetables. Chop finely or put through coarse blade of food chopper.
2. Put vegetables into large kettle; add vinegar, sugar, dry mustard, ginger, cinnamon, cloves, mace, and mustard seed, and red pepper (tied in cheesecloth).
3. Stir over medium heat until sugar is dissolved; increase heat and cook rapidly about 20 minutes, or until vegetables are tender. Stir frequently.
4. Immediately ladle into clean, hot jars. Seal, following manufacturer's directions.
5. Process in boiling water bath 10 minutes.

About 4 pints relish

Tomato Catsup

7 pounds ripe tomatoes (about 21 medium)
1 cup cider vinegar
1 cup sugar
1½ teaspoons paprika
1 teaspoon salt
½ teaspoon garlic salt
2 medium onions, sliced
1 clove garlic
½ cup coarsely chopped hot red pepper
1 piece (3 inches) stick cinnamon, broken in pieces
½ teaspoon whole cloves

1. Rinse tomatoes; plunge into boiling water, then into cold water. Peel and quarter tomatoes; remove as many seeds as possible.
2. Force tomatoes through a sieve or food mill. (There should be about 2 quarts pulp.)
3. Combine pulp in a large saucepot with the vinegar, sugar, paprika, salt, garlic salt, onion, and garlic.
4. Tie remaining ingredients loosely in a cheesecloth bag and add to tomato mixture. Bring to boiling over medium heat; reduce heat and simmer 1 hour, or until catsup is of desired consistency. Stir occasionally to prevent sticking to bottom. Remove cheesecloth bag.

5. Ladle into clean, hot jars. Seal, following manufacturer's directions.
6. Process in boiling water bath 5 minutes.

About 3½ pints catsup

Corn Relish

        6 cups prepared fresh corn or vacuum-packed
            canned corn
        1 cup chopped mild white onion
        1 cup chopped celery
        1 green pepper, chopped
        ¼ cup chopped pimento
        ½ to 1 cup sugar
        1 to 1½ tablespoons salt
        1 teaspoon crushed red pepper
        1 clove garlic, minced
        1 teaspoon celery seed
        ½ teaspoon ground ginger
        3 cups white vinegar
        1 to 1½ tablespoons dry mustard
        1 teaspoon ground turmeric
        3 tablespoons flour
        ¼ cup water

1. If using fresh corn on the cob, cook 5 minutes; plunge into cold water to cool thoroughly. Cut kernels from cobs (do not scrape cobs). If using canned corn, drain before measuring; set aside.
2. Combine onion, celery, green pepper, pimento, sugar, salt, red pepper, garlic, celery seed, and ginger in a large kettle; add 2½ cups of the vinegar and blend well. Bring mixture to boiling; boil 5 minutes.
3. Blend thoroughly the dry mustard, turmeric, and flour; stir in the water until smooth, then the remaining ½ cup vinegar. Stir into the hot mixture and cook about 6 minutes. Continue stirring until liquid is thickened and smooth.

4. Add the corn; cook and stir 5 minutes longer.

5. Ladle the hot relish into clean, hot jars. Seal, following manufacturer's directions.

6. Process in boiling water bath 15 minutes.

4 half-pints relish

JELLIES, JAMS, MARMALADES, PRESERVES, CONSERVES, AND BUTTERS

Homemade, old-fashioned, or just plain good—nothing says it better than a jar of sparkling jelly, plump and sweet preserves, or fruit-flecked marmalade.

The experienced cook knows that it doesn't take too much time or equipment to put up enough jars to capture fruits that will last through the winter months. And beginners will find jam or jelly making the perfect introduction to food preservation.

WHO'S WHO IN THE JELLY FAMILY

Jelly, jam, preserves, marmalade, conserve, butter—all are made from fruit, sugar, pectin and an acid. The finished product depends on the fruit itself, how you prepare and cook it, the amount of sugar used, and the proportions of other ingredients used.

Jelly is fruit juice that is jelled. Clear and sparkling, it holds its shape when turned out of the glass or cut, but it is tender enough to spread. Just-right jelly quivers a little.

Jam is made from whole, cut, or crushed fruit and includes both juice and pulp. Jam has enough body to hold its shape when spooned or spread, but it is softer and more flowing than jelly.

Marmalade is jelly with slices, shreds, or pieces of fruit captured in it. Citrus fruits are favorites for marmalade.

Preserves are small fruits, whole or in pieces, cooked in heavy syrup until plump, tender, and shiny.

Conserve is like jam, but made from a combination of fruits, one of them often a citrus. Nuts and raisins are traditional conserve ingredients.

Butters are very thick spreads made from cooked fruit that has been sieved, sweetened, and cooked, often with spices, until thick.

INGREDIENTS

Sugar is the preservative ingredient for jellies, jams, and their cousins: marmalades, butters, conserves, and preserves. Sugar is necessary for jell formation and, of course, for sweetness. You may use honey or corn syrup for a part of the sugar: honey for one-half the amount of sugar in the recipe, corn syrup for up to one-third the amount of sugar.

Pectin is what makes jelly jell. Pectin is a natural substance found in fruits. Some fruits—apples, crab apples, currants, blackberries, gooseberries, grapes, plums, raspberries, and citrus fruits—have enough natural pectin in them to jell without any assistance. Commercial pectin, made from fruit, helps jell fruits that are short on pectin. Dry and liquid pectin are handled differently because they are two entirely different products. Powdered pectin is added to juice or fruit before cooking; liquid pectin goes in after cooking. Our recipes and those on packaged pectin products give you sure-to-succeed directions. Don't try to substitute one form of pectin for the other—use the type the recipe calls for.

Underripe fruit has more pectin than very ripe fruit, so if you are not using commercial pectin, it is best to select a mixture of ripe and not-quite-ripe fruits. One-fourth unripe fruit to three-fourths ripe is a good balance. If using commercial pectin, select all ripe fruit.

Acid from tart fruits, lemon juice, or citric acid adds flavor and helps form the jell. Each recipe gives the proper amount of acid to add, so follow directions carefully.

Fruit for jelly-making should be really fresh. Pick or purchase fruit, keep refrigerated, and use as soon as possible. Jelly- or jam-making is a good way to use too large, too small, or unevenly shaped fruits that wouldn't be their prettiest when canned or frozen. You may use canned, frozen, or dried fruits or unsweetened canned juice or frozen juice concentrates for jam and jelly-making, too. Look to the recipes that follow for specifics.

Time is an important ingredient, too. Schedule your day so that you can complete the entire jam- or jelly-making process at one time. Preparing jams or jellies is not something you can start, then leave and pick up again several hours or even several minutes later. Work at a time when you expect the fewest interruptions. If you must stop to answer the phone or bandage a small knee, always take the pot off the heat before you leave!

PREPARATION

Jelly and all its family members are made by the open kettle method. Fruit, sugar, acid, pectin, and spices are cooked until ready to jell or until thick and of the desired consistency. Then the liquid and fruit are carefully poured or ladled into hot, clean (sterile for jelly) jars and sealed with lids (paraffin for jelly).

PROCESSING

Jelly needs no further processing once it is sealed in sterile jars. However, if using jars with two-piece self-sealing lids, it is a good idea to process for 5 minutes as indicated below for jams and other preserves. Jams, preserves, marmalades, and conserves should be processed in a boiling water bath at simmering temperatures (180°-185°F) for the times given in the recipes that follow. Check back to "Boiling Water Bath Step by Step," page 22, to refresh your memory on the boiling water bath process.

STORAGE

Store jams, jellies, and the like just as you do canned goods (see page 20), in a dark, cool, dry place. Refrigerator-freezer jams, as the name implies, are kept in the refrigerator or freezer.

CONTAINERS

Standard half-pint and pint canning jars and jelly glasses or jars are considered the safest and best containers for jellies, jams, etc. Although other containers are sometimes used, they are not recommended because they may not be able to withstand the extreme temperatures of boiling hot jelly and of sterilizing. Check all jars and lids to be sure they are flawless. Discard any defective lids or jars. Wash jars well and rinse with hot water. Keep jars for jams, marmalades, preserves, conserves and butters hot, but do not sterilize—the boiling water bath processing takes care of that. Jars and glasses for jelly must be sterilized, because jelly is not processed in the boiling water bath.

To sterilize jars, put a rack or folded dish towel in the bottom of a large pot. Put clean jelly jars or glasses on the rack, pour in boiling water to cover, and boil 15 minutes. Add boiling water, if necessary, to keep jars covered. Keep them hot in the kettle until ready to fill. Wash and rinse lids and bands. Follow manufacturer's directions for any additional preparation.

EQUIPMENT

The right equipment is just as important for jelly-making as the right ingredients. Always read through the

For successful jelly making, have the right equipment and the right recipe.

recipe and get out the necessary pots, pans, and utensils before you start. Here is a list of basic equipment:

large kettle (8 to 20 quarts) with a broad bottom for boiling juice and fruit (see A above)

large metal spoon for skimming foam (B)

wooden spoon for smooth, silent stirring (C)

sieve and/or colander for straining juice and fruit (D)

jelly bag (See instructions for how to make one on page 115.) (E)

standard glass canning jars and lids or jelly glasses or jars (F)

paraffin (household wax) to seal jellies (G)

double boiler, or other container to set over water, in which to melt the paraffin (H)

timer to keep track of processing times (I)

candy thermometer to check doneness (J)

wide-mouth funnel, for filling of jars (K)

ladle for filling jars (L)

dry and liquid measures (M_1 and $_2$)

clock with a second hand to time boiling
sharp knives, a masher, and a grater may also
come in handy

To make a jelly bag, simply cut a double thickness of
cheesecloth about 36 inches long, and fold it in half.
Dip it in hot water and then wring dry. Put a large
strainer or colander over a large bowl or saucepot and
place the cheesecloth in the strainer or colander. Pour
fruit or juice into the cheesecloth. Pick up the four
corners of the cloth bag and tie firmly. Let the bag rest
in the strainer, or hang it up, and let the juice drip
through.

To make a spice bag, cut a double thickness of cheesecloth about 5 inches square. Put whole spices in center
and tie corners firmly together.

Put fruit into jelly bag in colander; let stand until all
juice has collected into a pan below.

PERFECT JELLY STEP BY STEP

1. Reread recipe and gather all equipment.

2. Wash fruit well with cold water. Cut out any blemishes or bad spots. Remove stem and blossom parts.

3. Crush or cook fruit to extract juice. Berries need only to be mashed; firmer fruits should be cooked with just enough water to prevent fruit from sticking. Simmer just until tender. Do not overcook.

4. Pour fruit into jelly bag in a colander or strainer or hang the bag from a special stand, cupboard door handle, or from a broom handle placed across two chair backs. Let stand until all juice has dripped into a bowl or pan.

5. Meanwhile, prepare jars and lids following directions above.

Melt paraffin in double boiler, never over direct heat. Cover jelly with an 1/8-inch layer of paraffin.

6. If using paraffin, melt over low heat in a double boiler or coffee can or other container set over hot water. *Never* melt paraffin over direct heat. It is very flammable and could be dangerous.

7. Measure juice and prepare recipe as directed. (If there is a lot of pulp left in the bag, put it through a sieve or food mill and save to make fruit butter.)

8. Boil the juice, sugar, and any other ingredients in a *large* kettle—the mixture must boil rapidly and that takes plenty of space. Cook no more than 4 to 6 cups of juice at one time.

9. Follow the recipe directions for cooking time. Commercial pectin recipes usually boil for just 1 minute. If not using commercial pectin, boil for 2 minutes and then start testing for doneness. (See "Testing for the Jelly Point.")

10. Remove at once from heat; skim off foam with slotted or metal spoon and discard foam. (Some jellies may foam a lot while boiling. If so, skim while they boil as well as at end of cooking.)

11. Drain jars or remove from heat only as ready to use. Set jars right side up on rack or folded towel, away from drafts.

12. Carefully pour or ladle jelly into prepared hot glasses or jars to within ½ inch of top, if sealing with paraffin, or to within ⅛ to ¼ inch of top if using self-sealing lids.

13. Wipe inside edges and rims of jars with clean damp cloth, then dry.

14. Seal jars. Omit paraffin if using self-sealing lids, and follow manufacturer's directions. If using paraffin, pour enough melted paraffin on top of jelly to make a layer about ⅛ inch thick. This is about 1 tablespoon for a standard 6-ounce glass with a diameter of 2½ inches. Carefully tilt glass to distribute paraffin evenly and seal it to the edge of the glass. Prick any air bubbles in the paraffin.

15. Let jars cool on rack or on cloth, away from drafts, with enough space between jars for air to circulate.

JELLY WITHOUT ADDED PECTIN

Apple Jelly

1. Use tart, firm apples; about 3 pounds for a batch of jelly. About one-fourth of them should be underripe. Sort and wash; do not pare or core. Remove stems and blossom ends; cut apples into small pieces.

2. Add 1 cup water per pound of apples in a kettle. Cover; bring to boil on high heat. Reduce heat; simmer until apples are tender, about 20 to 25 minutes, depending on ripeness of the apples.

step by step

3. Put cooked apples into jelly bag and allow to drip, or press to remove juice. Strain pressed juice through two thicknesses of damp cheesecloth without squeezing.

4. Measure 4 cups of the apple juice into a large kettle. Add 3 cups of sugar and, if desired, 2 tablespoons of lemon juice. Stir to dissolve the sugar.

Continued

5. Boil mixture on high heat to 8°F above the boiling point of water, or until jelly mixture sheets from a spoon. Remove from heat. Skim off foam.

6. Pour into hot, sterile jars, to ½ inch from top; add an ⅛-inch paraffin layer. Or fill canning jars to ⅛ inch from top; wipe rims. Tightly screw on clean lids with sealing compound next to glass.

16. When cool, wipe jars with clean damp cloth to remove any spills on outsides. Check lid seals as manufacturer directs. Cover paraffin-sealed jars with metal lids, foil, or waxed paper.

17. Label, then store in cool, clean, dry, dark place.

TESTING FOR THE JELLY POINT

There are three methods to test jelly:

The jelly or sheet test. Remove pan from heat, dip spoon into boiling liquid, then lift out and tip so that the liquid can run over edge of spoon. When the last few drops in the spoon run together or "sheet" over the edge, the jelly is done.

Temperature. When thermometer in jelly mixture reaches 8° above boiling, the jelly is done. (At sea level, this would be 220°F. Measure temperature of boiling water with a thermometer to see what boiling temperature is where you live.)

Chill test. Remove pan from heat, spoon a small amount of liquid into a chilled plate or saucer, and put in freezer for a few minutes. If liquid jells, jelly is done.

JAMS, MARMALADES, PRESERVES, CONSERVES, AND BUTTERS

To make jams, marmalades, preserves, conserves, and butters, follow the same basic principles as outlined for jellies. In addition, however, these products must be processed in a boiling water bath at simmering temperatures (180°-185°F) to prevent spoilage. *Always* follow the recipe.

These products all have pieces of fruit in them, so they must be stirred constantly while cooking, to prevent sticking. Stirring is important just after cooking is completed, too. It helps the fruit to stay in suspension and prevents it from floating in the jars. Some cooks like

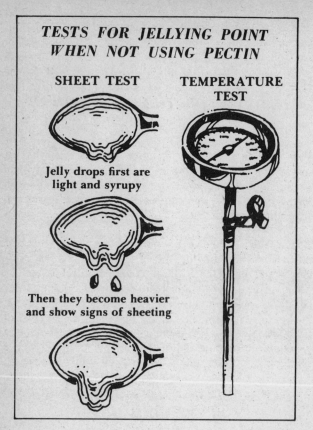

TESTS FOR JELLYING POINT WHEN NOT USING PECTIN

SHEET TEST   **TEMPERATURE TEST**

Jelly drops first are
light and syrupy

Then they become heavier
and show signs of sheeting

to let cooked fruit stand for 5 minutes, stirring often,
before pouring into jars and sealing. Skimming before
each stir is a good idea, too.

Jams, marmalades, and the like will thicken some as
they cool. Keep that in mind as you judge thickness of
the cooked mixture.

Here are some special tips for each type of product.

Jam. If not adding commercial pectin, test jams for
doneness with a thermometer. Temperature should

be 9°F above boiling. Or test by spooning a small amount of the fruit mixture onto a chilled plate and putting in the freezer to see if it holds its shape. Remember to take the pot off the heat while you test. Grandma tested jam for doneness by drawing a spoon across the center of the mixture in the pan. If it left a trail that didn't fill in immediately, the jam was thick enough.

Marmalade. Marmalades made with citrus fruits are old-time favorites. Remember that the white portion of citrus peel is bitter and use it with discretion. The peel does have pectin, so it is important to cook some. Citrus seeds have pectin, too. Tie them in a cheese-cloth bag and cook along with fruit.

Conserve. Nuts are frequently added to conserves, and their flavors are best if you add the nuts just 5 minutes before the end of cooking time.

Preserves. When making preserves, add sugar to fruit gradually to keep the fruit from shrinking. Hard fruits are usually precooked to soften them before sugar or syrup is added. You can heat the fruit in syrup and then let it stand in the syrup several hours or overnight to plump them up before finishing the cooking. Select fruits that are ripe but firm for preserves.

Butters. Watch butters carefully and stir them often because it is easy to overcook these thick fruit mixtures.

Freezer Jams and Jellies. These products are a relatively new and easy way to capture and save the wonderful flavors of fruits. These jams or jellies are not cooked, so they must be stored in the refrigerator or freezer. They will keep up to three weeks in the refrigerator, six months in the freezer. Follow recipe directions exactly, using commercial pectin.

JAM WITH POWDERED PECTIN

Peach Jam

1. Sort and wash fully ripe peaches. Remove stems, skins, and pits.

2. Crush or chop the peaches. A stainless steel potato masher is useful for this purpose.

step by step

3. Measure 3¾ cups of crushed peaches into a large kettle.

4. Add 1 package powdered pectin and ¼ cup lemon juice. Stir, dissolving the pectin. Over high heat, bring quickly to a full boil with bubbles over the entire surface.

Continued

5. Stir in 5 cups sugar, continue stirring and heat again to boiling. Boil hard for 1 minute, stirring constantly. Remove from heat; skim and stir alternately for 5 minutes to help prevent fruit from floating.

6. Pour jam into hot glasses to ½ inch from top. Cover at once with an ⅛-inch layer of paraffin. Cool, then cover jars with metal or paper lids. Label and store in a cool, dry place.

VOLUME EQUIVALENTS

1 gallon = 4 quarts
1 quart = 4 cups
1 pint = 2 cups
1 cup = 16 tablespoons
1 tablespoon = 3 teaspoons

WHAT WENT WRONG?

If your jelly did not turn out perfectly, these answers to common jelly-making complaints should help.

Did not set	Too much sugar, cooked too slowly, or not enough acid or pectin. Use as syrup or ice cream topping.
Soft	Not cooked enough, not enough sugar, not enough acid, or maybe too big a batch. Sometimes you can add more pectin and cook the jelly mixture again, or use for syrup.
Weeps	Too much acid or too much pectin, stored in too warm a place, overcooked, or too thick a layer of paraffin on top.
Cloudy	Squeezed jelly bag, some pulp got through bag, let jelly stand too long before pouring into jars, poured into jars too slowly, or used green fruit which set too fast.
Tough	Overcooked, too little sugar, or too much extra pectin.
Gummy	Overcooked.

Dark on top	Imperfect seal, or stored in too warm a place.
Crystals	Too much sugar, too little acid or pectin, over- or undercooked, or evaporation from standing uncovered.
Red jellies turn brown	Stored in too light a place, or stored in too warm a place.
Ferments	Containers not sterile, stored in too warm or too damp a place, or imperfect seal.
Mold	Imperfect seal, containers not sterile, or stored in too damp a place. If there is only a small amount of mold, just cut it off and discard.

Apple Jelly

    4 pounds tart apples
    4 cups water
      Sugar
      Paraffin

1. Rinse, remove stem ends, and quarter apples. (Do not core or pare fruit.) Add the water to apples in a large kettle. Cover and cook gently until fruit is soft, stirring occasionally.
2. Strain fruit through a jelly bag. The pulp remaining in the bag may be used to make apple butter, if desired.
3. To prepare jelly, measure not more than 4 cups of apple juice into saucepan. Measure ¾ cup sugar for each cup of juice. Heat the juice to boiling and stir in the sugar. Return to boiling and cook rapidly until mixture tests done.
4. Remove from heat; skim off foam.

5. Pour into hot, sterilized glasses. Seal with paraffin or lids, following manufacturer's directions.

5 half-pints jelly

Mint Jelly

Follow recipe for Apple Jelly; add **1 to 2 tablespoons mint juice** and **few drops green food coloring** when nearly done.

Mint juice: wash **2 cups fresh mint leaves** and cut very finely. Add **1/2 cup water** and **1/2 cup sugar** and let stand several hours. Heat to boiling, then strain.

Quick Sparkling Jelly

    1 quart bottled apple juice
    ½ envelope (about 1 tablespoon) strawberry-
        flavored soft drink mix
    1 box (1¾ ounces) powdered fruit pectin
    4¼ cups sugar
    Paraffin

1. Blend apple juice, drink mix, and pectin in a large heavy saucepot; stir over high heat until mixture comes to a full boil.
2. Add the sugar all at once and blend thoroughly. Bring to a full rolling boil; boil 1 minute, stirring constantly.
3. Remove jelly from heat; let stand several minutes and skim off foam.
4. Pour jelly into hot, sterilized glasses. Seal with paraffin or lids, following manufacturer's directions.

7 half-pints jelly

Blueberry Jelly

> 1 large lemon, sliced
> 3 quarts blueberries
> 3 pounds tart apples
>   Sugar (about 4½ cups)
>   Paraffin

1. Add enough water to lemon slices to just cover (about 1 cup.) Cover and refrigerate 12 hours, or overnight.
2. Pick over blueberries, discarding blemished berries. Rinse and drain. Turn into a saucepot.
3. Wash apples; remove stems, blossom ends, and blemished portions. Quarter the apples and put into a kettle; cover with water (about 2½ cups). Cook, covered, over medium heat until apples are soft.
4. Drain the liquid from lemon slices and mix with blueberries (discard lemon peel). Cook gently until blueberries are soft and juice flows freely.
5. Pour both fruit mixtures into a jelly bag; let drain 6 to 12 hours. (There should be about 6 cups juice.)
6. To make jelly, measure juice and pour half into a 2-quart saucepan and bring rapidly to boiling. For each cup of juice add ¾ cup sugar and stir until sugar is dissolved. Continue cooking rapidly until mixture tests done.
7. Remove from heat; skim off any foam. Pour jelly into hot, sterilized glasses. Repeat step 6 using remaining juice.
8. Seal with paraffin or lids, following manufacturer's directions.

About 7 half-pints jelly

Currant Jelly

    4 pounds (about 4 quarts) ripe red currants
    1 cup water
    4 cups sugar
    Paraffin

1. Rinse, remove leaves (not the stems), drain, and put currants into a kettle. Crush them thoroughly and stir in the water.
2. Bring rapidly to boiling; reduce heat and simmer, covered, 10 minutes. Strain through a jelly bag.
3. Measure 4 cups juice into a saucepan and bring rapidly to boiling. Add sugar and stir until dissolved; continue cooking rapidly until mixture tests done.
4. Remove from heat; skim off any foam.
5. Pour jelly into hot, sterilized glasses. Seal with paraffin or lids, following manufacturer's directions.

About 6 half-pints jelly

Crab Apple Jelly

Follow recipe for Currant Jelly. Omit currants. Rinse, remove stem ends, and cut into quarters enough **crab apples** to yield 3 quarts. (Do not core or pare the fruit.) Increase water to 3 cups and cook 20 minutes, or until apples are very tender. Decrease sugar to 3 cups.

Grape Jelly

Follow recipe for Currant Jelly. Omit currants. Rinse, remove stems, and drain **3 pounds Concord grapes.** Add water as for Currant Jelly but simmer, covered, 15 minutes. Decrease sugar to 3 cups.

Savory Grapefruit Jelly

½ cup boiling water
2 tablespoons dried savory
1 cup unsweetened grapefruit juice
3¼ cups sugar
Few drops green food coloring
½ of 6-ounce bottle liquid fruit pectin
Paraffin

1. Pour boiling water over savory in a small saucepan; cover tightly and set aside 10 to 15 minutes. Strain herb brew through fine strainer or cheesecloth into a measuring cup; add enough water to make ½ cup. Discard savory.
2. Pour herb brew into a 4-quart kettle or saucepan. Add grapefruit juice and sugar; stir over medium heat until sugar is dissolved.
3. Increase heat and bring mixture to boiling. Stir in food coloring and then pectin. Return to boiling; boil rapidly 1 minute, stirring constantly.
4. Remove from heat; skim off foam.
5. Pour into hot, sterilized glasses. Seal with paraffin or lids, following manufacturer's directions.

About 3 half-pints jelly

Mint-Honey Jelly

¾ cup boiling water
2 tablespoons dried mint leaves
2½ cups strained honey
Few drops green food coloring
½ of 6-ounce bottle liquid fruit pectin
Paraffin

1. Pour boiling water over mint in a saucepan; cover

tightly and let stand 15 minutes. Strain and add enough water to make ¾ cup. Discard mint.

2. Add honey and heat to boiling. Stir in coloring to tint a light green. Add pectin, stirring constantly. Bring to full rolling boil.

3. Remove from heat; skim off foam.

4. Pour into hot, sterilized glasses. Seal with paraffin or lids, following manufacturer's directions.

About 4 half-pints jelly

Pineapple Jelly

2¼ cups unsweetened pineapple juice
¼ cup lemon juice
4½ cups sugar
1 bottle (6 ounces) liquid fruit pectin

1. Measure pineapple juice and lemon juice into a large kettle; add sugar and mix well.

2. Bring rapidly to boiling, stirring constantly. Stir in pectin and bring to a full rolling boil; boil vigorously 1 minute, stirring constantly.

3. Remove from heat; skim off any foam.

4. Pour into hot, sterilized jelly glasses; seal with melted paraffin. (If jelly is to be used within 2 months, omit the paraffin.)

5. Cover glasses with lids, waxed paper, or aluminum foil, and store in refrigerator.

About 5 half-pints jelly

Basil Grape Jelly

½ cup boiling water
1 tablespoon dried basil
1½ cups bottled grape juice
3½ cups sugar
½ of 6-ounce bottle liquid fruit pectin
Paraffin

1. Pour boiling water over basil in a small saucepan; cover tightly and set aside 10 to 15 minutes. Strain herb brew through fine strainer or cheesecloth into a 4-quart kettle or saucepan. Discard basil.

2. Add grape juice and sugar to the kettle; stir over medium heat until sugar is dissolved. Increase heat and bring mixture to boiling.

3. Stir in the pectin and return to boiling; boil rapidly 1 minute, stirring constantly. Remove from heat; skim off foam.

4. Pour into hot, sterilized glasses. Seal with paraffin or lids, following manufacturer's directions.

About 4 half-pints jelly

Wine Jelly I

Topped with snowy-white whipped paraffin, this jelly becomes an attractive gift item.

    4 cups sugar
    1 box (1¾ ounces) powdered fruit pectin
    ¾ cup water
    3 cups wine (Madeira, rosé, or champagne)
    Snow Topping

1. Measure sugar; set aside.

2. Thoroughly mix pectin and water in a large saucepan. Bring rapidly to boiling over high heat and boil 1 minute, stirring constantly.

3. Reduce heat to medium and immediately add wine and all the sugar; keep mixture just below the boiling point and stir until the sugar is dissolved, about 5 minutes. Remove from heat.

4. If necessary, skim off foam with a metal spoon. Quickly pour jelly mixture into hot, sterilized jelly glasses. Cover at once with Snow Topping.

About 5 half-pints jelly

Note: If using champagne, the recipe will make about 4 glasses of jelly. Yield is less because the bubbling of champagne results in a great deal of foam loss.

Snow topping

Melt **2 bars paraffin** over boiling water. Pour a thin layer over hot jelly, using about 1 tablespoon melted paraffin for each glass. Cool remaining paraffin until it becomes cloudy and starts to solidify. Quickly whip with a rotary beater or a fork until paraffin is foamy and starts to harden. Work quickly. (If paraffin becomes too hard, melt and start again.) Spoon over the thin layer of paraffin on the jelly. Makes enough for about 6 jelly glasses.

Note: A 1-pound package of paraffin, also called household wax, contains 5 bars.

Wine Jelly II

3 cups sugar
2 cups wine*
½ of 6-ounce bottle liquid fruit pectin
Snow Topping (on this page)

1. Measure sugar and wine into the top of a double boiler; mix well. Place over rapidly boiling water and stir until sugar is dissolved, about 2 minutes. Remove from heat.
2. At once stir in pectin and mix well. Skim off foam, if necessary.
3. Quickly pour jelly mixture into hot, sterilized glasses. Cover at once with Snow Topping.

About 4 half-pints jelly

Note: This recipe may be doubled, if desired.

---

* Use sherry, Burgundy, sauterne, port, muscatel, claret, Tokay, or fruit wines—loganberry, currant, blackberry.

Cherry-Plum Jam

    2 pounds dark sweet cherries
    10 medium red plums
    1 cup water
    1 tablespoon lemon juice
    Sugar
    1 box (1¾ ounces) powdered fruit pectin

1. Rinse, stem, halve, and pit the cherries. (There should be about 1 quart fruit.)
2. Rinse, halve, and pit the plums. (There should be about 3½ cups fruit.)
3. Mix fruits, water, and lemon juice in a kettle. Bring to boiling, stirring occasionally; reduce heat and cook gently 3 minutes.
4. Remove from heat; measure mixture and return to kettle. For each cup of cooked fruit, add an equal amount of sugar. Stir until thoroughly blended.
5. Stir in the pectin and return to heat. Bring rapidly to full rolling boil, stirring constantly; boil and stir 2 minutes.
6. Remove from heat; skim off any foam. Ladle into clean, hot jars and seal, following manufacturer's directions.
7. Process by simmering in boiling water bath for 10 minutes.

10 half-pints jam

Pineapple-Strawberry Jelly-Jam

    2½ cups whole fresh strawberries
    1 can (12 ounces) unsweetened pineapple juice
    3 tablespoons lemon juice
    1 box (1¾ ounces) powdered fruit pectin
    4 cups sugar

1. Wash, hull, and quarter berries; measure 2 cups.
2. Mix berries, juices, and pectin in preserving kettle.

Place over high heat and stir until mixture comes to a full boil.

3. Stir in the sugar and return to rolling boil; boil vigorously 1 minute, stirring constantly.

4. Remove from heat; skim off foam.

5. Pour into hot sterilized jars or glasses. Seal with paraffin or lids, following manufacturer's directions.

About 6 half-pints jelly-jam

Rosy Banana Peach Jam

1 cup mashed fully ripe bananas (about 3 medium)
3¼ cups mashed fully ripe peaches (about 2 pounds peaches, peeled)
½ cup drained, chopped maraschino cherries
2 tablespoons lemon juice
6 cups sugar
1 box (1¾ ounces) powdered fruit pectin

1. Put prepared fruit and lemon juice into a large saucepan; mix.

2. Measure sugar into a bowl; set aside.

3. Mix pectin into fruit in saucepan. Stir and cook over high heat until mixture comes to a full rolling boil. Immediately add and stir in the sugar. Bring to a full rolling boil; stirring constantly, boil rapidly 1 minute.

4. Remove from heat; skim foam with metal spoon and then stir and skim for 5 minutes, to cool slightly and prevent floating fruit.

5. Immediately ladle into clean, hot jars, filling to within ½ inch of top. Seal immediately following manufacturer's directions.

6. Process by simmering in boiling water bath for 10 minutes.

Spiced Plum Jelly

    4 pounds fully ripe, tart clingstone plums*
    1 cup water
 6½ cups sugar
    ½ teaspoon ground cinnamon
    ⅛ teaspoon ground allspice
    ½ of 6-ounce bottle liquid fruit pectin
    Paraffin

1. Rinse, halve, pit, and crush plums (do not peel). Place in a large saucepan; add the water. Bring to boiling; reduce heat and simmer, covered, 10 minutes.
2. Ladle mixture into a jelly bag, and squeeze out juice. Measure 4 cups of the juice into a very large saucepan. Mix in sugar and spices.
3. Stir over high heat until mixture comes to a full boil. Immediately stir in fruit pectin and bring to a full rolling boil; boil rapidly 1 minute, stirring constantly.
4. Remove from heat; skim off foam.
5. Pour at once into hot, sterilized glasses. Seal with paraffin or lids, following manufacturer's directions.

About 10 half-pints jelly

Pineapple-Rhubarb Jam

    1 package (16 ounces) frozen rhubarb, thawed
    1 can (20 ounces) crushed pineapple
    1 teaspoon grated orange peel
    ½ teaspoon grated lemon peel
    2 tablespoons lemon juice
    6 cups sugar
    ½ of 6-ounce bottle liquid fruit pectin
    Few drops red food coloring

1. Combine rhubarb, pineapple, orange peel, lemon peel, and lemon juice in a large, heavy saucepan. Add

---

* If using sweet plums or freestone purple plums, use 3½ cups prepared juice and add ¼ cup lemon juice.

sugar and mix thoroughly. Bring to full rolling boil over high heat and boil rapidly 1 minute, stirring constantly.

2. Remove from heat; stir in pectin and food coloring. Skim foam, then stir about 10 minutes to cool jam slightly and keep fruit in suspension.

3. Ladle jam into clean, hot jars and seal, following manufacturer's directions.

4. Process by simmering in boiling water bath for 10 minutes.

7 half-pints jam

Citrus Marmalade

    1 large grapefruit
    2 medium oranges
    1 medium lemon
      Sugar
    ¼ cup fresh lemon juice

1. Wash the fruit. Slice into thin cartwheel slices. Cut grapefruit cartwheels into thirds, orange and lemon into halves.

2. Measure the fruit into a large kettle and add 1 cup water for each cup fruit. Bring to boiling; boil 20 minutes.

3. Remove from heat and measure the hot mixture; return to kettle and bring to boiling.

4. Remove from heat and add ¾ cup sugar for each cup of fruit and juice. Stir with a wooden spoon until thoroughly blended.

5. Return to heat and return to boiling. Boil 20 to 25 minutes, or until mixture tests done.

6. Just before removing from heat, stir in lemon juice.

7. Ladle into clean, hot glasses and seal, following manufacturer's directions.

8. Process by simmering in boiling water bath for 10 minutes.

6 half-pints marmalade

Peach and Mango Jam

2 cups sliced ripe peaches
2 cups sliced ripe mangos
3 cups sugar
¼ cup lemon juice

1. Combine peaches, mangos, and sugar in a heavy saucepan; cook over very low heat 1 hour, stirring frequently.
2. Blend in the lemon juice and continue cooking about 45 minutes, or until thickened.
3. Ladle into clean, hot jars and seal, following manufacturer's directions.
4. Process by simmering in boiling water bath 10 minutes.

3 to 4 half-pints jam

Red Raspberry Jam
(Refrigerator-Freezer Type)

1½ cups sieved fresh red raspberries (about 3 cups
      whole berries)
3 cups sugar
¼ cup bottled fruit pectin

1. Mix the sieved raspberries and sugar together in a bowl. Let stand for 20 minutes.
2. Add the fruit pectin to the raspberry mixture and mix thoroughly.

3. Immediately fill clean, hot jars or glasses; seal and set aside until jam is set, 24 to 48 hours.

4. Store in refrigerator to use within 2 or 3 weeks. Store in freezer if kept longer.

About 4 half-pints jam

Strawberry Jam
(Refrigerator-Freezer Type)

   4 cups sugar
   2 cups crushed ripe strawberries (about 2 pints)
   ¾ cup water
   1 box (1¾ ounces) powdered fruit pectin

1. Add sugar to crushed strawberries in a large bowl; mix well and set aside.

2. Combine the water and pectin in a small saucepan; blend well. Bring to boiling and boil 1 minute, stirring constantly. Stir into sweetened strawberries. Continue stirring about 3 minutes. (There will be some sugar crystals remaining.)

3. Ladle jam into clean, hot jars; seal immediately and set aside until jam is set, 24 to 48 hours.

4. Store in refrigerator to use within 2 or 3 weeks. Store in freezer if kept longer.

5 half-pints jam

Strawberry-Mint Jam

Follow recipe for Strawberry Jam. Add **1 or 2 drops mint extract** to each jar before filling. Stir quickly to blend. Cover immediately.

Strawberry-Cardamom Jam

Follow recipe for Strawberry Jam. Mix **2 teaspoons ground cardamom** with the sugar and add to straw-berries; blend well.

Peach Marmalade

   3 pounds (about 12 medium) firm, ripe peaches
   1 orange
   3 cups sugar

1. Plunge peaches into boiling water to loosen skins; plunge into cold water and gently slip off skins.
2. Halve and pit the peaches; coarsely chop enough to yield 4 cups.
3. Wash the orange; cut off ends and thinly slice; discard seeds.
4. Combine peaches, orange, and sugar in a large saucepot; stir over medium heat until sugar is dissolved. Increase heat and cook rapidly until clear and thick, stirring frequently to prevent sticking. (Cooking time will vary with degree of ripeness and type of peach.)
5. Remove from heat and skim off any foam. Ladle into clean, hot jars and seal, following manufacturer's directions.
6. Process by simmering in boiling water bath for 10 minutes.

3 half-pints marmalade

Blackberry Jam
(Refrigerator-Freezer Type)

   3 cups mashed or sieved blackberries
      (about 3 pints)
   5½ cups sugar
   1 box (1¾ ounces) powdered fruit pectin
   1 cup water

1. Mix the berries and sugar in a bowl; let stand 20 minutes, stirring occasionally.
2. Blend the pectin and water in a large saucepan; bring to boiling and boil rapidly 1 minute, stirring con-

stantly. Remove from heat; add the berry-sugar mixture and stir about 2 minutes.

3. Ladle into clean, hot jars, seal immediately, and set aside 24 to 48 hours, or until the jam is set.

4. Store in refrigerator to use within 2 or 3 weeks. Store in freezer if kept longer.

7 half-pints jam

Lime Marmalade

   4 medium limes
   2 medium lemons
     Sugar

1. Wash and dry the fruit. Cut through peel and pulp into very thin slivers; discard seeds.

2. Measure the fruit and juice into a large bowl. (There will be about 2½ cups.) Add 3 times the amount of water. Cover and set aside overnight.

3. The next day, turn the mixture into a large kettle and bring rapidly to boiling; reduce heat and simmer about 30 minutes. Return to the bowl, cover and set aside overnight.

4. The third day, measure the mixture into a heavy saucepan or kettle. (There will be about 6 cups.) For each cup add ¾ cup sugar; mix well.

5. Cook gently over low heat until the mixture thickens. (See tips for jam on page 122.)

6. Ladle into clean, hot jars and seal, following manufacturer's directions.

7. Process by simmering in boiling water bath for 10 minutes.

5 half-pints marmalade

Holiday Treat Preserves

    4 cups (1 pound) cranberries
    2 cups (about 3 small) pears, diced
    1 can (13¼ ounces) pineapple tidbits, drained
        (reserve ¼ cup syrup)
    ½ cup water
    2 cups sugar

1. Wash, drain, and sort cranberries.
2. Rinse, halve, core, pare, and dice enough pears to yield 2 cups. Sprinkle reserved pineapple syrup over pears.
3. Mix water and sugar in a saucepan; stir over medium heat until boiling; cover and boil gently 5 minutes. Add the cranberries and cook, uncovered, until all the skins burst.
4. Add the pears with syrup and drained pineapple. Continue cooking until thick, about 20 minutes. Remove from heat; skim off any foam.
5. Ladle into clean, hot jars and seal, following manufacturer's directions.
6. Process by simmering in boiling water bath for 10 minutes.

5 half-pints preserves

Spiced Orange Wedges

   12 oranges
    4 cups sugar
    3 pieces (2 inches each) stick cinnamon, broken
       in pieces
1½ teaspoons whole allspice

1. Cut each orange into 6 wedges. Put into a large bowl. Add **water** to cover (about 1 quart). Let stand 3 to 4 hours. Drain oranges, reserving oranges and 1 quart of liquid.

2. Combine liquid, sugar, and spices in a large saucepan. Bring to boiling; boil 5 minutes. Add oranges; return to boiling, reduce heat, and simmer, uncovered, 20 minutes, or until skins are slightly transparent.

3. Pack oranges and spices into clean hot jars. Fill jars with hot syrup to within ½ inch of top. Remove air bubbles and add more hot syrup, if needed, to fill jars to within ½ inch of top.

4. Seal, following manufacturer's directions.

5. Process in boiling water bath 15 minutes.

6. Serve as a meat accompaniment.

8 half-pints spiced oranges

Cantaloupe Preserves

    1 large, unripe cantaloupe
    1 quart water
    2 cups sugar
    ½ lemon, thinly sliced
    2 tablespoons thinly sliced crystallized ginger

1. Cut cantaloupe into wedges, discarding seedy portion. Pare wedges and cut orange portion into 1-inch pieces. (There should be 3½ to 4 cups cantaloupe pieces.)

2. Cover cantaloupe in a bowl with a salt solution (1 tablespoon salt dissolved in 2 quarts cold water). Cover and let stand 8 hours, or overnight.

3. Drain cantaloupe in a colander and rinse with cold water. Put into a large saucepan and cover with boiling water; cook 8 to 10 minutes, or until cantaloupe is tender, but not soft. Drain thoroughly.

4. Meanwhile, mix the water and sugar in a saucepan. Bring to boiling, stirring until sugar is dissolved; boil, uncovered, about 5 minutes. Add the cantaloupe, lemon, and ginger. Cook rapidly until cantaloupe is translucent, 30 to 40 minutes. Remove from heat; cover tightly and set aside.

5. The next day, reheat the preserves to boiling and

ladle into clean, hot jars. Seal immediately, following manufacturer's directions.

6. Process by simmering in boiling water bath for 10 minutes.

4 half-pints preserves

Prize Strawberry Preserves

   3 cups fresh, firm, ripe strawberries
   3 cups sugar

1. Rinse, hull, and drain berries thoroughly on absorbent paper. Halve the very large berries. Put into a heavy saucepan.

2. Add 1 cup sugar; stirring gently, bring to boiling. Boil 5 minutes, stirring constantly.

3. Repeat step 2 twice more, using remaining 2 cups sugar and boiling 5 minutes after each addition.

4. Turn into shallow glass dish, cover, and let stand 24 hours. Stir occasionally while cooling.

5. Ladle into clean, hot jars and seal, following manufacturer's directions.

6. Process by simmering in boiling water bath for 10 minutes.

3 half-pints preserves

Brandied Orange Halves

   6 large oranges
   1 tablespoon salt
   4 to 5 quarts boiling water
   6 cups sugar
   6 cups water
   1 cup brandy

1. Put whole oranges and salt into a kettle with enough boiling water to cover. Bring to boiling; boil, uncovered, 10 minutes. Drain and rinse. Cut oranges in half, crosswise.

2. Combine sugar and 6 cups water in a clean kettle. Bring to boiling; add orange halves. Simmer gently, uncovered, 20 minutes and turn occasionally. Cover; let cool in syrup 4 to 6 hours.

3. Reheat oranges in syrup to boiling. Simmer, uncovered, 5 minutes. Cover; let stand overnight.

4. Measure 2 cups of the syrup and pour into a saucepan. Bring to boiling and boil briskly about 10 minutes, or until reduced to 1 cup. Add brandy; cover and keep warm.

5. Bring oranges to boiling in remaining syrup; keep hot. Using one clean hot pint jar at a time, pack with 3 orange halves and ½ cup hot brandied syrup. Add enough hot syrup from kettle to fill jar to within ⅛ inch of top. Seal, following manufacturer's directions.

6. Allow to mellow at least 6 weeks before using.

7. To serve, scoop pulp from orange halves; chop into pieces with some of the peel and syrup. Spoon over pound or sponge cake, gingerbread, puddings, or ice cream. Orange shells may be rolled in sugar, allowed to dry, and used as cups for fancy desserts.

4 pints preserved fruit

Best-Ever Tomato Preserves

    1 pound tart green apples
    4 pounds firm, ripe tomatoes
    2 lemon slices, ¼ inch thick
    4 cups sugar
      Red food coloring (optional)

1. Wash, pare, quarter, core, and cut apples into small cubes. (There should be about 3 cups.)
2. Rinse, scald, peel, and cut tomatoes into small pieces. (There should be about 2 quarts.)
3. Mix apples, tomatoes, and lemon in a large kettle. Bring to simmering over medium heat and stir in the sugar. Cook gently, uncovered, until of desired consistency, about 1½ hours. Stir occasionally as the mixture begins to thicken.
4. If desired, stir in several drops of red food coloring.
5. Ladle preserves into clean, hot jars. Seal, following manufacturer's directions.
6. Process by simmering in boiling water bath for 10 minutes.

4 half-pints preserves

Fresh Pineapple Preserves

    2 medium fresh pineapples (about 2 pounds each)
      Sugar

1. Cut off spiny tops and rinse the pineapples. Cut into ½-inch crosswise slices. With a sharp knife, cut away and discard the rind and "eyes" from each slice. Cut out the core and cut slices into small wedges.
2. Measure 4 cups of the pineapple wedges and 3 cups sugar. Place half the fruit into a bowl and cover with half the sugar. Repeat layers with remaining fruit and sugar. Cover bowl tightly and set aside overnight.
3. The following day, drain the pineapple syrup into a

saucepan, reserving the pineapple. Bring syrup to boiling and boil 1 minute. Remove from heat and add drained pineapple. Turn the mixture into a shallow heat-resistant dish and set aside to cool.

4. Ladle cooled preserves into clean, hot jars and seal, following manufacturer's directions.

5. Process by simmering in boiling water bath for 10 minutes.

3 half-pints preserves

Stuffed Pears

    3¾ pounds small, firm-ripe fresh Bartlett pears
    1¾ cups sugar
    1½ cups water
    ⅓ cup lemon juice
    1 stick cinnamon
    ½ cup chopped golden raisins
    2 tablespoons chopped maraschino cherries
    Whole maraschino cherries

1. Select pears of good shape.

2. Combine **1 gallon cold water** and **2 tablespoons** each **salt and vinegar** in a bowl.

3. Pare pears and core from the bottom using a ¼ teaspoon measure or small melon baller. Drop pears into the water to prevent darkening while preparing remaining fruit and the syrup.

4. Combine sugar, water, lemon juice, and cinnamon in a kettle large enough to hold pears in a single layer. Heat to boiling, stirring until sugar is dissolved. Cover and simmer 10 minutes.

5. Drain and rinse pears with cold water. Mix raisins and cherries; stuff into core cavities. Press whole cherry into the opening of each pear. Put pears into boiling syrup; cover and cook gently about 8 minutes.

6. Pack pears carefully into clean, hot, wide-mouth quart jars and fill jars with hot syrup to within ½ inch of top. Remove air bubbles and add more syrup, if needed, to fill to within ½ inch of top.

7. Seal, following manufacturer's directions.

8. Process in boiling water bath 25 minutes.

2 quarts preserved fruit

Nectarine Pineapple Conserve

2½ pounds fresh nectarines
1 can (8¼ ounces) crushed pineapple
¼ cup lemon juice
¼ cup chopped maraschino cherries
7½ cups sugar (3 pounds)
½ of a 6-ounce bottle liquid fruit pectin

1. Pit nectarines, but do not peel. Finely chop or grind, using coarse blade. (Or, put about ½ cup diced nectarine at a time into an electric blender container and blend at chop or low speed just until finely crushed.) Fruit should measure 3 cups.

2. Combine crushed nectarines, undrained pineapple, lemon juice, cherries, and sugar in a large kettle. Heat to boiling, stirring until sugar is dissolved. Boil vigorously 1 minute. Remove from heat and immediately stir in pectin. Stir and skim off foam for 7 minutes.

3. Ladle mixture into clean hot jars and seal, following manufacturer's directions.

4. Process in boiling water bath at simmering for 10 minutes.

9 half-pints conserve

Cranberry Conserve

> 4 cups (1 pound) fresh cranberries
> 1 cup water
> 1 cup dark seedless raisins, chopped
> 2½ cups sugar
> 1 tablespoon grated orange peel
> ⅓ cup orange juice
> 1 cup coarsely chopped walnuts or other nuts

1. Wash and drain cranberries.
2. Put cranberries into a saucepan and add water; bring to boiling and cook, uncovered, 5 minutes, or until all the skins burst.
3. Force cranberries through a sieve or food mill. Combine purée in a saucepan with the raisins, sugar, orange peel, and orange juice; mix well. Stir over medium heat until sugar is dissolved, then continue cooking about 15 minutes, or until thick.
4. Remove from heat; stir in walnuts. Ladle into clean, hot jars and seal, following manufacturer's directions.
5. Process by simmering in boiling water bath for 10 minutes.

3 half-pints conserve

Spicy Nectarines

> 4 pounds fresh nectarines
> 2 cups sugar
> 1 cup water
> ¾ cup vinegar
> 1 whole nutmeg, cracked
> 4 small bay leaves
> 4 lemon slices
> 4 lime slices

1. Pour boiling water over nectarines and let stand a minute. Drain and slip off skins. Cut fruit from pits into quarters.

2. Combine sugar, water, vinegar, and nutmeg in a saucepan. Bring to boiling, stirring until sugar is dissolved. Cover and simmer 10 minutes. Add nectarine quarters, return to boiling, and cook 2 minutes.

3. Pack fruit into clean, hot jars, adding a bay leaf, lemon slice, and lime slice to each jar. Fill jars with hot syrup to within ½ inch of top. Remove air bubbles and add more syrup, if needed, to fill to within ½ inch of top.

4. Seal, following manufacturer's directions.

5. Process in boiling water bath 20 minutes.

4 pints preserved fruit

Note: If desired, nectarines may be packed raw (uncooked) into hot jars and boiling syrup added to fill jars. Increase processing time to 25 minutes. When packed raw, less fruit but more syrup is needed. Either use syrup and boiling water to fill or prepare one and a half times the syrup recipe.

Brandied Nectarines

4 pounds fresh nectarines
1 cup sugar
1¼ cups water
4 whole cloves
1 pod cardamom
1½ tablespoons sliced preserved or candied ginger
4 orange slices
1 cup brandy

1. Pour boiling water over nectarines and let stand a minute. Drain and slip off skins. Cut fruit in halves and remove pits.

2. Combine sugar, water, cloves, seeds from cardamom pod, and ginger in a saucepan. Bring to boiling, stirring until sugar is dissolved. Cover and simmer 10 minutes.

Add nectarine halves and bring to boiling. Cover and cook 5 minutes.

3. Pour ¼ cup hot syrup into each clean, hot jar. Fill with nectarines and 1 orange slice. Add ¼ cup brandy to each jar. Fill jars with hot syrup to within ½ inch of top. Remove air bubbles and add more syrup, if needed, to fill to within ½ inch of top.

4. Seal, following manufacturer's directions.

5. Process in boiling water bath 20 minutes.

4 pints preserves

Banana-Pecan Butter

3 cup crushed ripe bananas (6 to 7 medium)
1 teaspoon grated lemon peel
¼ cup lemon juice
6½ cups sugar
½ teaspoon butter or margarine
1 bottle (6 ounces) liquid fruit pectin
1 cup pecans, chopped

1. Combine the bananas, lemon peel, lemon juice, sugar, and butter in a large heavy saucepan; blend thoroughly.

2. Bring to boiling and boil 2 minutes, stirring constantly to prevent sticking.

3. Remove from heat; stir in pectin and chopped pecans. Ladle into clean, hot jars and seal, following manufacturer's directions.

4. Process by simmering in boiling water bath for 10 minutes.

8 half-pints fruit butter

Grape Butter

2 pounds Concord grapes
4½ cups sugar

1. Rinse the grapes; discard stems and blemished grapes. Drain and put into a large heavy saucepot. Add

sugar and mix thoroughly. Stir over medium heat until sugar is dissolved. Increase heat and cook rapidly 20 minutes, stirring frequently to prevent sticking.

2. Remove from heat and force grape mixture through a coarse sieve or food mill.

3. Return the pulp to saucepot and bring to boiling over high heat, stirring constantly. Boil rapidly 1 minute.

4. Remove from heat and skim off any foam. Ladle into clean, hot jars and seal, following manufacturer's directions.

5. Process by simmering in boiling water bath for 10 minutes.

About 5 half-pints fruit butter

Cherry-Tomato Conserve

    4 large tomatoes, peeled and chopped
 1½ cups sugar
    1 medium onion, chopped
    1 green pepper, chopped
    1 lemon, thinly sliced
    1 teaspoon ground ginger
    1 jar (8 ounces) red maraschino cherries, drained
        and chopped
  ½ cup nuts, chopped

1. Mix tomatoes and sugar together in a saucepan. Let stand 3 hours, or until sugar is dissolved; stir occasionally.

2. Add onion, green pepper, lemon slices, and ginger; mix well. Bring to boiling. Reduce heat and simmer until thick, 1½ to 2 hours, stirring occasionally.

3. Remove from heat and mix in cherries and nuts. Ladle mixture into clean, hot jars and seal, following manufacturer's directions.

4. Process by simmering in boiling water bath for 10 minutes.

3 half-pints conserve

Moselem Springs Apple Butter

A favorite Pennsylvania Dutch recipe.

16 medium tart apples (about 6 pounds)
2 quarts water
1½ quarts apple cider
3½ cups sugar
1 teaspoon ground cinnamon
1 teaspoon ground allspice
1 teaspoon ground cloves

1. Wash and cut the apples into small pieces. (There should be about 4 quarts.) Cover with the water in a large kettle and cook, covered, until apples are soft, stirring occasionally.
2. Press through a coarse sieve or food mill to remove skins and seeds.
3. Bring cider to boiling in a heavy saucepot; stir in the apple pulp and sugar. Cook and stir over medium heat until sugar is dissolved. Reduce heat and cook slowly until mixture thickens, stirring occasionally to prevent sticking.
4. Blend in a mixture of the spices and continue cooking until apple butter is of spreading consistency.
5. Ladle into clean, hot jars and seal, following manufacturer's directions.
6. Process by simmering in boiling water bath for 10 minutes.

About 4 pints apple butter

Lebanon County Rhubarb Preserves

2½ pounds rhubarb
3½ cups sugar
2 to 2½ tablespoons grated orange peel
¾ cup orange juice

1 Wash rhubarb and cut into small pieces. Peel stalks

if skin is tough. Combine in a saucepan with the sugar, orange peel, and orange juice.

2. Stir over low heat until sugar is dissolved, then bring to boiling over medium heat. Reduce heat and cook slowly until mixture thickens, about 30 minutes, stirring occasionally.

3. Ladle into clean, hot jars and seal, following manufacturer's directions.

4. Process by simmering in boiling water bath for 10 minutes.

About 3 pints preserves

Ginger-Apricot Conserve

    1 pound dried apricots
 2½ cups water
    7 cups sugar
    ½ cup thinly sliced crystallized ginger
    1 cup thinly sliced Brazil nuts

1. Cover apricots with the water in a heavy saucepan; set aside 1 hour. Stir in sugar and ginger.

2. Bring to a rolling boil over medium heat; reduce heat and cook gently 15 to 20 minutes, or until of desired consistency. Stir occasionally to prevent sticking.

3. Stir in the nuts and remove from heat; skim off any foam. Pour into clean, hot jars; seal following manufacturer's directions.

4. Process by simmering in boiling water bath for 10 minutes.

8 half-pints conserve

FREEZING

Freezing is an easy, quick, safe, and good way to preserve food. It's economical, too, if you go about it correctly.

Freezing keeps all those things we look for in food—flavor, color, vitamins, and minerals. In fact, if you hurry fresh foods into your freezer, they are likely to retain more nutritive value than foods that wait in the market for hours or perhaps days.

Freezing food is an investment. In addition to the money you spend to buy and operate the freezer and on the food and packaging materials, you are spending time, too.

Take some of that time right now to learn the whys and hows of freezing, to make yourself a knowledgeable investor. Preparing, processing, or packaging food the wrong way could cost you food and time. Doing it the right way saves you time and money, and good eating is the dividend!

THE FREEZER

Go get the use and care booklet or instruction manual that came with your freezer and read it again. It is important to understand this major appliance, how it works, what it can and can't do for you. You'll learn how to load your freezer, how full to fill it, and how to defrost.

PLANNING FREEZER USE

How you fill your freezer is determined by your own needs and your family's food preferences, as well as by when and how often they eat, how and how often you entertain, whether you have a garden, and whether you like to cook and bake ahead. Give some thought to how you want your freezer to work for you.

Using freezer space wisely is one of the best lessons a freezer-cook can learn. Keep your freezer at least two-thirds full—it will operate more efficiently and cost less to run and still leave room for short-term storage, or to add specials.

Look to your freezer instruction manual to see what load your freezer can accommodate. A general rule is not to add more than 2 to 3 pounds of food per cubic foot of freezer space during any 24-hour period. That means a 20-cubic-foot freezer can take 60 pounds of food every 24 hours.

If you have a lot of food to freeze (and enough freezer space to store it), take food to a locker plant to be frozen. Once frozen, take it home to your own freezer to store.

Rotation and inventory may sound like terms a warehouse manager or purchasing agent would use. Your freezer is a warehouse and you are indeed a purchasing agent, so rotation and inventory are important for you. First in, first out is a standard rule of inventory and of freezing. Use the oldest foods in the freezer first and keep your stock moving.

How do you know which is the oldest food? Clear and accurate labeling is one way. Always label all foods with type of food, any information about its preparation, number of servings or size or weight of contents, date put in freezer, and date to use by.

An inventory listing is another help. Keep a clipboard with a list of the foods in the freezer hanging from the door handle or wall near the freezer. Write down how much of which food went in when, then check it off when you take it out. It needn't be a sophisticated system, just one that is easy for you to use.

FOODS FOR FREEZING

The foods your family likes and eats often are obvious choices to fill your freezer. Seasonal foods, to be prepared and frozen at the peak of their goodness, are another easy choice. Lower prices or special sales can save you money when you have a freezer to store the specials.

Convenience foods and short-term storage items may merit space in your freezer. These include frozen entrees, complete dinners, desserts, vegetables, baked goods, ice cream, lunch box specials, party favorites, herbs, and many other foods. (See "Freezer Tips," page 165.) Select perfect, high-quality foods for freezing, because what you select is what you get. Freezing, just as canning, does not improve food—it can only save what you have.

There are many varieties of fruits and vegetables that have been developed especially for freezing. Your fruit stand manager should know, or you can get advice from your state extension service.

Freeze foods in small amounts. Buy and prepare only the amount of food you can handle. Your time and the freezer space you have available determine how much you buy.

PREPARATION

Shop for freshness and then handle foods quickly and carefully to preserve them. After you have selected the very best foods, rush them home and prepare quickly and carefully, following recipe directions. If possible, prepare and freeze foods just as soon as you get them home from the garden or market. If they must wait, refrigerate them at once and keep there until ready to prepare.

Foods going into the freezer should be frozen quickly to retain their flavor, color, and nutritive value. Prepare, package, and put right into the freezer. If you can't get them into the freezer immediately, refrigerate until you can.

Cleanliness is just as important in freezing as it is in canning or any other food preparation. Freezing does not kill bacteria—it only freezes them. Once thawed they can get right back to work to spoil food and make people sick, so a clean cook, clean equipment, and clean work surfaces are musts!

PROCESSING

Vegetables *must* be blanched (briefly precooked) in boiling water or steam, then chilled, before freezing. Blanching stops enzyme activity, helps retain vitamins, and helps green vegetables stay green. If not blanched, foods can lose flavor and quality. You may hear claims that blanching isn't necessary, but you will be taking a

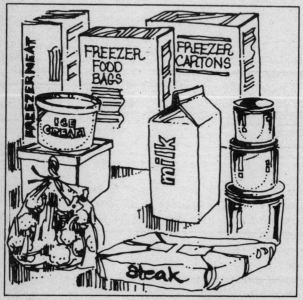

Proper packaging is essential for success in freezing.

chance on poor flavor, texture, and nutrition if you skip this step. See "Blanching Step by Step" on page 170 for blanching directions.

PACKAGING

What's on the outside of foods wrapped for freezing is as important as what's inside. Proper packaging materials and proper packaging procedures make the difference between good foods and bad. Buy good quality packaging products and always follow the manufacturer's directions.

Freezer packaging products *must* be moisture and vapor proof to preserve flavor, color, texture, and vitamins. You can select freezer paper, heavy-duty plastic or plastic bags, heavy-duty foil, rigid plastic containers with tight-fitting lids, waxed cartons with plastic bags that fit inside, or tapered freezing jars.

The food itself determines the packaging you use. Rigid containers or bags in boxes are necessary for liquids or semiliquids. Meats and large pieces of food can be wrapped in freezer paper or heavy-duty foil. Loosely packed fruits and vegetables are fine frozen in heavy plastic bags.

Don't forget that you want to neatly pack all these containers into a square or rectangular space. Packages with corners fit and stack better than tub-shaped containers.

Sealing edges of containers must be kept clean. Wipe rims of rigid containers with a damp cloth or paper towels; be sure plastic bag openings are clean.

You need to allow headspace when packing foods, because they will expand as they freeze. Dry packed foods need about ½-inch headspace; liquids or semiliquids ½ to 1 inch, depending on the size of the opening at the top of the container (small opening needs more headspace). Crumpled plastic wrap or freezer paper placed on top of fruit in syrup helps to hold fruit under syrup and prevent discoloration.

Packages must be sealed airtight. If they aren't, air

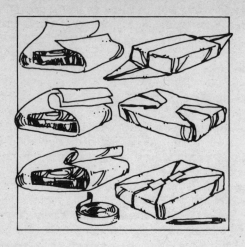

Two methods of packaging: A drugstore wrap for meat and airtight plastic wrap for vegetables.

will get in, the food will lose moisture and flavor, and the result is freezer burn. Some foods can discolor as well.

Freezer tape is a must for sealing freezer-paper wrapped packages and to run around rims of rigid containers. Twist ties, string, or rubber bands should be used to close plastic bags. Zip-sealing plastic bags seal themselves. You may use heavy boil-in-bags that come with their own heat-sealing device.

Follow these steps to package foods in freezer paper, plastic wrap, or foil.

1. Tear off enough wrap to go around food 1½ times.
2. Place food in center of sheet.
3. Bring edges of wrap together, fold over at the top and crease.
.4. Fold over and over until last fold is tight against food.
5. Smooth and press the fold from center out to ends to press out air.
6. Fold ends to point, then fold each end under to seal.
7. Turn package over, bring ends up and seal tight with freezer tape.
8. Label and freeze.

Follow these steps to package foods in sealing bags.

1. Pack food in bags.
2. Squeeze air out. Leave headspace, if recipe directs.
3. Twist top of bag, then turn top back.
4. Twist tie, rubber band, or tie string over doubled twist of bag.
5. Label and freeze

Always pack foods in package sizes that are appropriate for your family. Remember that smaller packages freeze, and thaw, faster.

Many foods—green beans, corn on the cob, sliced carrots, whole small fruits—can be frozen individually on cookie sheets, trays, or shallow pans, covered with waxed paper. When frozen solid, pack in containers or bags. Then you just shake out the amount you need, close the bag, and tuck it back in the freezer.

TEMPERATURE

Freeze and store foods at 0°F or lower. Keep a freezer thermometer in your freezer and check it whenever you add or take out food.

Read the instruction manual for your freezer to see if you can adjust the temperature, if necessary. Also check to see where the coldest part of your freezer is. In chest freezers, walls are the coldest. Shelves of upright freezers are coldest. Foods to be frozen should be placed in those areas.

Leave room for air to circulate between packages of foods being frozen. Arrange in a single layer, if possible, and away from already frozen foods. Once food is frozen, you can stack it and move to other parts of the freezer.

Try to open the freezer door only when necessary. Cold air is lost each time the door is opened, especially with an upright model. Frost build-up on walls, shelves, and packages means that freezer temperatures are fluctuating, so check the thermometer and the traffic.

EMERGENCIES

If your freezer stops working, check fuses, plug, and instruction manual before calling the service man. If there is a mechanical or power failure *don't open the freezer!* If the freezer is fairly full and has been at 0°F, the food will not start to thaw for 12 to 20 hours, *if* door is kept closed.

If power will be off for more than a day, move food to another freezer (a neighbor's or a locker). If the freezer is full and food thaws, the freezer will not re-freeze all the food in it before some starts to spoil.

If you can't move food to another freezer, use dry ice to keep the food cold. A 50-pound chunk, put in soon after the freezer stops, will keep food frozen for 2 to 3 days.

If food has begun to thaw, check it carefully. It is safe to refreeze or to cook if it has not gotten above refrigerator temperature (40°F). Some flavor and quality may be lost, but it is safe to eat. Use refrozen foods as soon as possible and heat thoroughly before serving.

If foods have reached a temperature above 40°F, *do not* refreeze and *do not* eat them. Thawed ground meats, poultry, or fish that look or smell bad should be discarded. Thawed ice cream should not be used either.

Any food that looks or smells questionable is better discarded. Remember, when in doubt, throw it out. It's not the refreezing that's dangerous, but the bacterial growth that might have begun while the food was above 40°F.

FREEZER TIPS

Use your freezer to quick-cool pie fillings and gelatin molds or mixtures.

Store marshmallows in plastic bags in the freezer. Cut while frozen and they won't stick!

Nuts store best in the freezer, retaining flavor and texture.

Brown sugar, if freezer-stored, won't get hard or lumpy.

Keep your candle supply in the freezer. They will keep their pretty shape and burn more brightly.

Dry cereals and whole grain flours and cereals stay fresher in the freezer.

Freeze cooked rice in meal-sized portions, then reheat in colander or sieve over boiling water.

Freeze cornmeal mush just as soon as you've tipped it out of its loaf pan mold. Slice while still frozen and fry right away—no need to thaw.

Buy citron and candied fruits during the holidays when they are plentiful to freezer-store for those times when they are not readily available.

MAXIMUM TIME LIMITS

General time limits (in months except as noted)
for storing frozen foods at 0°F or lower.

BAKED AND COOKED FOODS

Breads, yeast, baked	2 to 4
bakery (in original wrap)	less than 1
quick, baked	1 to 3
unbaked	2 weeks
rolls, baked	2 to 3
brown and serve	2 to 3
unbaked	less than 1
Cakes, frosted	1 to 2
unfrosted	2 to 3
batters	less than 1
cupcakes	2 to 3
fruitcakes	12
Cookies, baked	9
dough	9
Pies, baked	2 to 3
unbaked	3 to 4
chiffon	1
pastry shells	2
Sandwiches	less than 1
Stews, soups, prepared main dishes	2 to 3
Leftover cooked foods	1

FRUITS AND VEGETABLES   8 to 12

DAIRY PRODUCTS

Creamery butter, Cheddar cheese	4 to 5
Cottage cheese (not creamed)	4 to 6
Cream (40%)	3 to 4
whipped	1
Eggs, whole and yolks	12
whites	9
Ice cream	1 to 2
Milk (homogenized)	1

FISH AND SHELLFISH

Fish, lean	6 to 8
fatty	3 to 4
salmon	2 to 3
Shellfish	4 to 6
shrimp, cooked, peeled	2 to 3
cooked, unpeeled	4 to 6

GAME
8 to 18

GAME BIRDS
8 to 12

POULTRY

Chicken, whole	6 to 8
cut up	4 to 6
giblets	1 to 3
Duckling, turkey	6 to 8
Goose	3 to 4

MEATS

Fresh, beef	6 to 12
veal	6 to 9
lamb	6 to 9
pork	3 to 6
ground beef, veal, lamb	3 to 4
ground pork	1 to 3
variety meats	3 to 4
Smoked ham, whole	2
Corned beef	2 weeks
Cooked, leftover	2 to 3
meat pies	3
Swiss steak	3
stews	3 to 4
Prepared meat dinners	2 to 6

NUTS

Salted	3
Unsalted	9 to 12

Buy frozen fruits in big containers (25 pounds), thaw only until you can separate pieces, then quickly repack in smaller containers and freeze at once. This is a great way to buy frozen fruit, especially if you bake a lot of pies.

Freeze too-ripe bananas, or buy to freeze if they're a bargain. Freeze in peel, then thaw and put right into cakes or bread. Or peel, mash with lemon juice (1 tablespoon per cup) and pack in containers, leaving 1-inch headspace. Seal and freeze.

Keep a cold stock pot for soups. Use a clean coffee can to collect leftovers that are not enough to make a meal in themselves: vegetable cooking water or leftover vegetables, tag ends of roasts, leftover cooked rice, pasta, etc. Just add them to the coffee can and return to freezer. Weeks or months hence, when the can is full, heat it up. Taste and season as necessary, perhaps adding a bouillon cube or two, more vegetables, some rice, pasta, or potatoes. One family calls it "Mystery Soup" and looks forward to its occasional appearance.

Save a corner of your freezer for ice to use for drinks, for quick-chilling of foods, and for ice-cream making. You can keep ahead of your ice needs by emptying trays of cubes into a heavy-duty plastic bag whenever you think of it.

Freeze surprises in ice cube trays: leftover coffee, tea, lemonade, or punch become cubes to chill glasses of these beverages. Drop lemon slices, mint sprigs, maraschino cherries, or tiny perfect flowers into water in ice cube trays and freeze for festivities. Water frozen in a ring mold is a pretty cooler for your party punch bowl.

Partly used jars of olives, pickles, cherries, or pimentos needn't turn to mold in the refrigerator. Just freeze them until you need them. Be sure there is plenty of headspace in the jar for liquid to expand as it freezes. Water chestnuts. bamboo shoots, and kraut from a can may also be frozen right in the liquid they come in.

Dried fruits wait very patiently in the freezer. Opened boxes of prunes, dates, raisins, figs, and even shredded or flaked coconut may get stale on the shelf or in the refrigerator, but not if carefully overwrapped and stored in the freezer.

FREEZING DO'S AND DON'TS

DO freeze only enough of seasonal foods to last until the next harvest.

DO cool foods quickly before freezing. Set pans of food in ice water; use cold syrup or water to chill fruits and vegetables.

DO get as much air out of packages or bags as possible.

DON'T refreeze food unless it has been cooked or has not gotten any warmer than refrigerator temperature (40°F).

DON'T freeze soft meringues (on pies, in frostings), custard or cream pies, layer cakes with soft fillings, or cake batters.

DON'T use lots of butter or fats when preparing foods for freezer. Fats tend to separate when frozen.

VEGETABLES

Pick fresh and tender vegetables for freezing. Vegetables that are high in water (lettuce, radishes, green onions, salad greens) are not recommended for freezing because they lose their texture and become limp.

Wash vegetables thoroughly in cold water. Scrub them, if necessary. Always lift vegetables out of water rather than letting dirty water drain off over them. Sort for uniform sizes so all pieces will cook in the same amount of time. Don't let vegetables stand in water—they will lose nutrients and flavor. All vegetables, except green peppers, must be blanched.

BLANCHING STEP BY STEP

1. You will need a blancher, or make one yourself with a wire basket or colander that fits inside a large kettle. The kettle must have a lid. Do not use copper or iron utensils for blanching.

2. Heat to boiling at least 1 gallon water for each pound of vegetables to be blanched. Keep water boiling all during blanching.

3. Put prepared vegetables in wire basket and lower into rapidly boiling water. (You can use a wire rack or cover to keep vegetables in the basket if kettle is very large.)

4. Cover at once and begin timing for time given in recipe. Add 1 minute to blanching time if you live above 5000 feet.

5. When time is up, immediately remove basket from blancher and immerse in very cold or ice water. (Fill sink or large kettle with water and several trays of ice cubes. Change water and add more ice as necessary to keep water very cold.)

6. Cool in cold water for same time as given for blanching.

7. Drain thoroughly.

8. Pack and seal.

9. Label and freeze.

STEAM-BLANCHING STEP BY STEP

Steam-blanching is recommended for broccoli, mushrooms, sweet potatoes, and winter squash.

1. Use a steamer or make one from a large kettle with a tight-fitting lid, a rack about 3 inches high that fits in the bottom of the kettle, and a wire or steaming basket.

2. Pour 1 to 2 inches of water into the kettle and heat to boiling.

3. Arrange a single layer of vegetables in the basket and place on rack in kettle.

4. Cover and steam for time given in the recipe. Steam 1 minute longer if you live above 5000 feet.

5. When time is up, immediately remove basket from steamer and immerse in very cold or ice water for the same time as given for blanching.

6. Drain thoroughly.

7. Pack and seal.

8. Label and freeze.

Asparagus

Wash and, if very gritty, remove or clean under scales. Sort by size and cut to size of container or into 2-inch pieces. Blanch small stalks 2 minutes, medium stalks 3 minutes, and large stalks 4 minutes. Chill, drain, and pack in containers. Alternate tip and stem ends in containers. Seal and freeze.

Beans, Green

Wash, remove ends, and sort by size. Pack small beans whole, french-cut medium beans, and cut large beans in 1- or 2-inch pieces. Blanch 3 minutes. Chill, drain, and

APPROXIMATE YIELD OF FROZEN VEGETABLES FROM FRESH

VEGETABLE	FRESH	FROZEN
Asparagus	24 lb. 1 to 1½ lb.	15 to 22 pt. 1 pt.
Beans, lima (in pods)	1 bu. (32 lb.) 2 to 2½ lb.	12 to 16 pt. 1 pt.
Beans, green and wax	1 bu. (30 lb.) ⅔ to 1 lb.	30 to 45 pt. 1 pt.
Beet greens	15 lb. 1 to 1½ lb.	10 to 15 pt. 1 pt.
Beets (without tops)	1 bu. (52 lb.) 1¼ to 1½ lb.	35 to 42 pt. 1 pt.
Broccoli	1 crate (25 lb.) 1 lb.	24 pt. 1 pt.
Brussels sprouts	4 quart boxes 1 lb.	6 pt. 1 pt.
Carrots (without tops)	1 bu. (50 lb.) 1¼ to 1½ lb.	32 to 40 pt. 1 pt.
Cauliflower	2 med. heads 1⅓ lb.	3 pt. 1 pt.
Chard	1 bu. (12 lb.) 1 to 1½ lb.	8 to 12 pt. 1 pt.
Collards	1 bu. (12 lb.) 1 to 1½ lb.	8 to 12 pt. 1 pt.

Corn, sweet (in husks)	1 bu. (35 lb.) 2 to 2½ lb.	14 to 17 pt. 1 pt.
Kale	1 bu. (18 lb.) 1 to 1½ lb.	12 to 18 pt. 1 pt.
Mustard greens	1 bu. (12 lb.) 1 to 1½ lb.	8 to 12 pt. 1 pt.
Peas	1 bu. (30 lb.) 2 to 2½ lb.	12 to 15 pt. 1 pt.
Peppers, sweet	⅔ lb.	1 pt.
Pumpkin	3 lb.	2 pt.
Spinach	1 bu. (18 lb.) 1 to 1½ lb.	12 to 18 pt. 1 pt.
Squash, summer	1 bu. (40 lb.) 1 to 1¼ lb.	32 to 40 pt. 1 pt.
Squash, winter	3 lb.	2 pt.
Sweet potatoes	⅔ lb.	1 pt.

pack in containers, leaving ½-inch headspace. Seal and freeze.

Note: Blanched and chilled beans may be spread out on waxed-paper-covered baking sheets to freeze. When frozen, pack loose in heavy plastic bags and seal.

Beans, Lima

Shell, wash, and pick over. Sort by size. Blanch small beans 2 minutes, medium beans 3 minutes, and large beans 4 minutes. Chill, drain, and pack in containers. Leave ½-inch headspace. Seal and freeze.

Beans, Soy

Use only green soybeans in pod. Wash. Blanch 5 minutes. Chill. Squeeze beans out of pod. Pack in containers. Leave ½-inch headspace. Seal and freeze.

Beets

Wash and sort by size. Cut off tops, leaving about 1 inch stem. Cook in boiling water until tender (20 to 25 minutes for small beets, 45 to 50 minutes for large); chill. Peel and slice or cube. Pack, leaving ½-inch headspace. Seal and freeze.

Broccoli

Wash, peel stalks, and trim. Split large stalks so tops are no more than 1½ inches across. Scald in steam 5 minutes or in boiling water 3 minutes. Drain, chill, and pack in containers, alternating tops and stems. No headspace needed. Seal and freeze.

Note: To remove insects, soak broccoli in salt water (4 teaspoons salt per gallon) for ½ hour.

Brussels Sprouts

Trim off outer leaves. Wash thoroughly. Sort by size. Blanch small sprouts 3 minutes, medium sprouts 4 minutes, and large sprouts 5 minutes. Drain, chill, and pack in containers. No headspace needed. Seal and freeze.

Carrots

Remove tops. Wash, peel, and slice or dice. Blanch 2 minutes if cut, 5 minutes if whole. Drain, chill, and pack, leaving ½-inch headspace. Seal and freeze.

Cauliflower

Trim off leaves. Wash, peel, and separate into flowerets. Blanch 3 minutes in boiling salted water (4 teaspoons salt to 1 gallon water). Chill, drain, and pack in containers. No headspace needed. Seal and freeze. (To remove insects, see recipe for broccoli.)

Corn on the Cob

Use freshly picked, young, tender ears and hurry them from the garden to the kitchen. Husk, remove silk, wash, trim tips, and sort by size. Blanch small ears 7 minutes, medium ears 9 minutes, and large ears 11 minutes. Chill. Package, seal, and freeze.

Corn, Whole Kernel

Prepare as for corn on the cob. Blanch small ears 3 minutes, medium ears 5 minutes, and large ears 7 minutes. Chill and drain. Cut kernels from cob. Pack in containers, leaving ½-inch headspace. Seal and freeze.

Eggplant

Pare and slice or dice. Blanch 4 minutes, adding ½ cup lemon juice to each gallon water used for blanching. Chill and drain. Pack in containers, leaving ½-inch headspace. Seal and freeze.

Greens (spinach, kale, beet tops, mustard greens, chard, collards)

Use only tender young leaves. Wash thoroughly. Discard thick stems and imperfect leaves. Blanch 2 minutes (3 minutes for collards). Chill and drain. Pack in containers, leaving ½-inch headspace. Seal and freeze.

Mushrooms

Sort by size. Wash and cut off tips of stems. Cook in butter or margarine 5 minutes; cool, pack in containers, leaving ½-inch headspace, and seal.

Or blanch in steam 3½ minutes for small whole mushrooms and 3 minutes for sliced mushrooms. Chill, drain, and pack in containers, leaving ½-inch headspace. Seal and freeze. If blanching in steam, drop in

BLANCHING

1. Use a blancher, or a wire basket inside a large kettle with a lid. Do not use copper or iron utensils for blanching.

2. For each pound of vegetables to be blanched, heat at least 1 gallon of water to boiling.

3. Put prepared vegetables in wire basket; lower into boiling water. If kettle is very large, hold vegetables down with lid or rack.

4. Cover at once; begin timing for time given in recipe. If you live above 5000 feet, add 1 minute to blanching time.

Continued

5. Remove basket from blancher as soon as time is up. Immerse in ice-cold water. Add ice cubes to water in sink to keep cold.

6. Allow as much time for cooling the vegetables in cold water as for blanching.

7. Drain vegetables thoroughly.

8. Pack into freezer containers, leaving no headspace.

Continued

9. Label, including name of vegetable and date. Freeze.

acid solution (2 cups cold water and 1 teaspoon lemon juice) for 5 minutes before steaming to prevent discoloration.

Onions

Peel and chop. Spread on cookie sheet and freeze. Pack in containers leaving ½-inch headspace or bag, seal, and freeze.

Peas

Shell, discarding hard or overmature peas. Blanch 1½ minutes. Chill and drain. Pack in containers, leaving ½-inch headspace. Seal and freeze.

Peppers, Green or Red

Wash, stem, halve, and seed. Chop, slice or dice, spread on cookie sheet, and freeze or pack in containers. No headspace needed. Seal and freeze.

Squash, Summer

Wash and cut in ½-inch slices. Blanch 3 minutes. Chill

and drain. Pack in containers, leaving ½-inch head-space. Seal and freeze.

Note: Squash slices may be spread out on waxed-paper-covered baking sheets to freeze. When frozen, pack loose in heavy plastic bags.

Squash, Winter, and Pumpkin

Wash, cut into pieces, removing seeds and fiber. Cook until tender by steaming, baking, or boiling, 15 to 20 minutes. Remove pulp and mash or sieve. Chill in refrigerator or by setting bowl or pan in ice water. Pack in containers leaving ½-inch headspace. Seal and freeze.

Tomatoes, Whole

Pick firm but ripe tomatoes. Wash well. Wrap individual tomatoes in plastic wrap and freeze. Or, wash tomatoes, core, and peel. Package, leaving 1-inch headspace. Seal and freeze.

Tomatoes, Stewed

Stem, peel, and quarter tomatoes. Simmer, covered, 10 to 20 minutes or until tender. Cool. Pack in containers, leaving ½- to 1-inch headspace. Seal and freeze.

Tomato Juice

Wash, sort, trim, and quarter firm but ripe tomatoes. Simmer 5 to 10 minutes. Press through sieve. If desired, add 1 teaspoon salt per quart of juice. Pour in containers, leaving ½- to 1-inch headspace. Seal and freeze.

Vegetable Purées

Vegetables frozen in puréed form save freezer space, and they are welcome additions to your baby's diet, to other special diets, to creamed soups, or to pies. Among the vegetables suitable for puréeing are asparagus, peas,

FREEZING GREEN BEANS

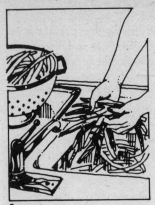

1. Select young, tender, stringless beans that snap when broken. Allow ⅔ to 1 pound of fresh beans for 1 pint frozen. Wash thoroughly.

2. Cut beans into 1- or 2-inch pieces, or slice them lengthwise.

step by step

3. Put beans in blanching basket, lower into boiling water, and cover. Heat for 3 minutes. Keep heat high under the water.

4. Plunge basket of heated beans into cold water to stop the cooking. It takes about as long to cool as to heat them. When the beans are cool, remove them from water and drain.

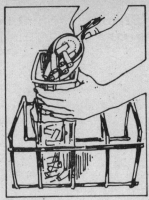

5. Pack the beans into bags or other containers. A stand to hold the bags makes filling easier. A funnel helps keep the sealing edges clean.

6. Leave ½-inch headspace. Seal, twisting and folding back top of bag and tying with string. Store at 0°F or lower at once. Bags may need outside carton for protection.

TIMETABLE FOR COOKING FROZEN VEGETABLES*

Time to allow after
water returns to boil†

VEGETABLE	MINUTES
Asparagus	5–10
Beans, lima:	
Large type	6–10
Baby type	15–20
Beans, snap, green, or wax:	
1-inch pieces	12–18
Julienne	5–10
Beans, soybeans, green	10–20
Beet greens	6–12
Broccoli	5–8
Brussels sprouts	4–9
Carrots	5–10
Cauliflower	5–8
Chard	8–10
Corn:	
Whole-kernel	3–5
On the cob	3–4
Kale	8–12
Kohlrabi	8–10
Mustard greens	8–15
Peas, green	5–10
Spinach	4–6
Squash, summer	10–12
Turnip greens	15–20
Turnips	8–12

* Use ½ cup of lightly salted water for each pint of vegetable with these exceptions: Lima beans, 1 cup; corn on the cob, water to cover.

† Time required at sea level; slightly longer time is required at higher altitudes.

FREEZING BROCCOLI

1. Trim off leaves and tough parts of stems; wash thoroughly. If needed, soak stalks for ½ hour in salt water (4 teaspoons salt to each gallon of water) to remove insects.

2. Cut broccoli lengthwise into uniform pieces, leaving heads about 1½ inches across to insure uniform heating and make attractive pieces for serving.

step by step

3. Place pieces in blanching basket over rapidly boiling water to steam. Cover kettle, steam 5 minutes over high heat. Or heat in boiling water 3 minutes, as is shown for green beans (page 171).

4. Remove basket from boiling water. Cool broccoli by plunging basket into cold water.

Continued

5. Lift basket from cold water as soon as broccoli is cool and let drain a few minutes.

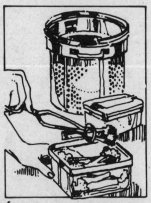

6. Pack broccoli so some heads are at each end of container. No headspace is needed. Press lid on firmly to seal. Freeze at once. Store at 0°F or below.

spinach, carrots, parsnips, rutabagas, turnips, sweet potatoes, and squash.

To freeze: Cook vegetables in boiling water or steam them, just as you prepare them for the table. When tender, drain and force through a sieve or food mill. Cool quickly. Spoon purée into freezer containers, allowing ¼- to ½-inch headspace; seal, label, and freeze.

To thaw: Place frozen block of purée in top of a double boiler and heat over simmering water.

COOKING FROZEN VEGETABLES

Frozen vegetables do not need to be thawed before cooking, except for corn on the cob. Heat a small amount of salted water to boiling (½ cup is usually enough; limas need 1 cup, corn on the cob needs enough to cover). Add vegetable, cover, and cook just until tender.

Vegetables packaged in boilable bags can be heated in bags in boiling water, as manufacturer directs. To cook vegetables in microwave oven, follow manufacturer's directions for utensils and times.

Squash and pumpkin are best reheated in the oven or over boiling water.

 # FRUITS

Preparing fruits for the freezer is just about as simple as preparing them for dessert!

Pick fresh, ripe, and unblemished fruits, choosing varieties that are recommended for freezing—your state agricultural extension service or county home economist can name them for you.

If you are not certain whether a fruit will freeze well, test-freeze a small quantity, say three or four packages. Sample the fruit after it has been in the freezer a few days to see whether you'll want to freeze it in large quantities.

ASCORBIC ACID SUBSTITUTION

Teaspoons of crystals or powder	=	Tablets
1/8 teaspoon		375 milligrams
1/4 teaspoon		750 milligrams
1/2 teaspoon		1500 milligrams
3/4 teaspoon		2250 milligrams
1 teaspoon		3000 milligrams

Crush tablets and dissolve in a small amount of cold water. Then add to chilled syrup just before pouring over fruit in containers.

PREPARATION

Wash fruits thoroughly in cold water. Handle carefully to prevent bruising. Always lift fruits out of water and then let water, and dirt, drain off.

Peel, pit, and cut or slice fruit, following recipe directions. Prepare only enough fruit at one time to fill a few containers.

Do not use galvanized iron or chipped enamel utensils to prepare fruit for freezing. The metal in these utensils will produce discoloration.

DARKENING AND DISCOLORATION

Many fruits will discolor when exposed to the air or during freezer storage, so take one of the following precautions.

1. Add 1½ to 2 teaspoons crystalline or powdered ascorbic acid to each gallon of chilled syrup just before using. You can use ascorbic acid (vitamin C) tablets in place of powder—see Ascorbic Acid Substitution chart.

2. Use commercially prepared ascorbic acid mixture, following manufacturer's directions.

3. Let fruit stand in acid-water (1 teaspoon lemon juice or ¼ teaspoon citric acid powder or crystals per quart of water) 2 minutes, then drain before packing in containers.

SWEETENING

Fruits can be packed dry without sugar, dry with sugar, or in syrup. Natural color and flavor are better if fruits are sweetened before freezing, but if you have a calorie counter in your house, pack fruits without sweetening.

Dry pack is good for blueberries, cranberries, pineapple, raspberries, and rhubarb. All you do is wash, drain, and prepare the fruit as the recipe directs; then spread it out on a waxed-paper-lined cookie sheet or tray. Freeze solid. When frozen, transfer the fruit to containers or bags, seal, and return to freezer. Since each piece is individually frozen, you can pour or shake out just what you need, then return the rest to the freezer. Individually frozen fruits thaw in less time than solid blocks, too.

Sugar pack is best for juicy fruits and sliced fruits, and it is the preferred way to pack fruits to be used for pies and other cooking. Just mix the fruit and sugar in a large bowl or other container before filling freezer containers. Or put the fruit in the containers and sprinkle sugar over it.

You will use about 1 cup of sugar for 4 cups of fruit. If you like it sweet, use 1 cup sugar to 3 cups fruit. To make it not so sweet, use 1 cup sugar to 5 cups fruit.

Syrup pack is preferred for fruits to be used as desserts and for fruits that discolor, because syrup covers the fruit, keeping out air. To hold fruit under the syrup, just put a small, crumpled piece of waxed or freezer paper on top of the fruit, then close and seal containers.

SYRUP HOW-TO

Combine sugar and water in the proportions given in the Syrup How-To chart and mix until sugar dissolves. Do not beat the syrup—you don't want any air bubbles. Chill syrup thoroughly before using. Make it the day before, if you can.

PACKAGING

Pack fruits for freezing in plastic bags or cartons or in containers with tight-fitting lids. Paper cartons that held milk, ice cream, or cottage cheese should not be used because they are not moisture-vapor-proof.

Leave headspace (room for food to expand as it freezes) as recipe directs, usually ½ inch for dry pack, ½ inch for 1 pint liquid, and 1 inch for 1 quart liquid.

Tapered freezer jars are fine to use, but do not use jars that do not have straight sides: they might break as food expands. Also it is very difficult to get food out of these containers.

Spoon fruit into containers, wiping any rims with a clean damp cloth or paper towel so they are clean to seal. Fit on lids. Seal plastic bags as directed on page

163. Rigid containers can be sealed with freezer tape placed over the edge of the lid.

THAWING

Thaw fruits in their containers, unopened, either in the refrigerator, at room temperature, or under cold running water, until defrosted enough that you can separate pieces. Fruit can still be icy cold.

A pint of frozen fruits takes half an hour or so to thaw under cold running water, 2 to 4 hours at room temperature, and 5 to 8 hours in the refrigerator. Refrigerator thawing gives the best results in flavor and texture.

Apples

Wash, pare, core, and slice apples about ½ inch thick. For syrup pack, slice directly into freezer containers of syrup (see below). For sugar pack, slice directly into salt water (2 tablespoons salt per gallon water); drain.

Sugar pack: Steam-blanch (page 171) apple slices about 2 minutes. Chill in cold water; drain. Add ½ cup sugar for each quart apple slices. Pack in containers, leaving ½-inch headspace. Seal and freeze.

Syrup pack: Add ½ teaspoon ascorbic acid to each quart 40% syrup. Use about 1 cup syrup per quart sliced apples, or enough to cover. Pack in containers, leaving ½- to 1-inch headspace. Seal and freeze.

Applesauce, Baked Apples

Prepare applesauce or baked apples from your favorite recipe; cool thoroughly. Pack in containers, leaving headspace, or in a bag. Seal and freeze.

Apricots

Wash, peel, halve, and pit.

SYRUP HOW-TO

Type of Syrup	Cups Sugar*	+	Cups Water	=	Cups Syrup
30%	2		4		5
40%	3		4		5½
50%	4¾		4		6½
60%	7		4		7¾

Note: You will need about ⅔ to 1 cup syrup for each quart of fruit.

If you wish to substitute dry sugar pack for syrup, follow this substitution table:

30% syrup	= 1 cup sugar to 5 cups fruit
40% syrup	= 1 cup sugar to 4 cups fruit
50% syrup	= 1 cup sugar to 3 cups fruit

Sugar pack: Add ½ cup sugar for each quart apricot halves. Pack in containers. Leave ½-inch headspace. Seal and freeze.

Syrup pack: Pack fruit in containers. Add ½ teaspoon ascorbic acid to each quart 40% syrup. Use about 1 cup syrup per quart apricot halves, or enough to cover. Leave ½- to 1-inch headspace. Seal and freeze.

Avocados

Select soft, ripe fruit. Wash, cut in half, pit, peel, and mash. Add 3 tablespoons lemon juice to each quart avocado purée. Pack in containers, leaving ½- to 1-inch headspace. Seal and freeze.

---

* Up to ¼ the total amount of sugar may be replaced by light corn syrup.

Blackberries

Wash and drain; handle as little as possible.

Dry pack: Freeze on cookie sheets or trays, then pack in containers or bags. Seal and return to freezer.

Sugar pack: Add ¾ cup sugar for each quart berries. Pack in containers, leaving ½-inch headspace. Seal and freeze.

Syrup pack: Pack fruit in containers. Cover with 40 or 50% syrup, leaving ½- to 1-inch headspace. Seal and freeze.

Blueberries (elderberries, huckleberries)

Wash, pick over, and drain. Discard stems and green berries.

Dry pack: Freeze on cookie sheets or trays, then pack in containers or bags. Seal and return to freezer.

Cherries, Sour

Wash, sort, stem, drain, and pit.

Sugar pack: Use ¾ cup to 1 cup sugar per quart pitted cherries. Pack in containers, leaving ½-inch headspace. Seal and freeze.

Syrup pack: Pack fruit in containers. Add ¼ teaspoon ascorbic acid to each quart 40% syrup. Use about 1 cup syrup per quart cherries, or enough to cover. Leave ½- to 1-inch headspace. Seal and freeze.

Cherries, Sweet

Wash, sort, stem, and drain. Not necessary to pit.

Syrup pack: Pack fruit in containers. Add ¼ teaspoon ascorbic acid to each quart 40% syrup. Use about 1

cup syrup per quart cherries, or enough to cover. Leave
½ - to 1-inch headspace. Seal and freeze.

Cranberries

Wash and sort. Discard stems and blemished berries.
Drain.

Dry pack: Freeze on cookie sheets and pack in containers or bags. Seal and return to freezer.

Syrup pack: Pack fruit in containers. Cover with 50%
syrup, leaving ½ - to 1-inch headspace. Seal and freeze.
Cranberries purchased in sealed moisture-vapor-proof
bags can be frozen as is. When ready to use, open bag
and wash and pick over berries. No need to thaw before chopping, grinding, or cooking.

Dry pack, sugar pack, and syrup pack methods of
freezing.

Citrus Fruits (grapefruit, oranges)

Wash, peel, and section over a bowl; discard membranes and seeds. Use juice as desired. Bag and freeze the peel to use to grate or shred.

Juice pack: Pack sections in containers and add juice to cover, leaving ½- to 1-inch headspace.

Syrup pack: Pack sections in containers. Add ½ teaspoon ascorbic acid to each quart 50% syrup. Use about 1 cup syrup per quart fruit sections, or enough to cover. Leave ½- to 1-inch headspace. Seal and freeze.

Citrus Fruit Juices (grapefruit, orange, lime, lemon)

Squeeze or extract juices, remove seeds, and strain, if desired. Sweeten with sugar, if desired. Add ¾ teaspoon ascorbic acid to each gallon of juice. Pour into containers, leaving ½- to 1-inch headspace. Lemon or lime juice can be frozen in premeasured amounts in ice cube compartments. When frozen, remove from compartments and pack in bags. Seal and return to freezer.

Frozen juice pops: Pour juice into small paper cups, insert wooden sticks, and freeze.

Fruit Cocktail

Use any combination of sliced or diced fruit, small whole fruits, or melon balls.

Syrup pack: Pack fruit in containers. Cover with 30% or 40% syrup, leaving ½- to 1-inch headspace. Seal and freeze.

Fruit Juices (apple, berry, cherry, grape, plum, rhubarb or cider)

Simmer fruits for 5 minutes in just enough water to prevent sticking. Drain through sieve or jelly bag. Freeze unsweetened, or add sugar to taste. Work quickly to retain vitamin C. Pack in containers, leaving ½ - to 1-inch headspace. Seal and freeze.

Grapes

Wash, sort, stem, and drain. Remove seeds, if necessary.

Dry pack: Freeze on cookie sheets or tray and pack in containers or bags. Seal and return to freezer.

Syrup pack: Pack fruit in containers. Cover with 40% syrup, leaving ½ - to 1-inch headspace. Seal and freeze.

Grape Juice

Wash, stem, and crush grapes. Strain through jelly bag (see page 115). Let stand overnight so sediment can settle. Pour clear juice off into containers, leaving ½ - to 1-inch headspace. Seal and freeze.

Melons

Wash, halve, and remove seeds. Cut in slices, cubes, or balls.

Dry pack: Freeze on cookie sheets or trays; then pack in containers or bags. Seal and return to freezer.

Syrup pack: Pack fruit in containers. Cover with 30% syrup, leaving ½ - to 1-inch headspace. Seal and freeze.

Juice pack: Pack fruit in containers along with whole, seedless grapes. Cover with orange juice. Leave ½ - to 1-inch headspace. Seal and freeze.

Peaches

Wash, peel, halve, and pit peaches.

Syrup pack: Add ¼ teaspoon ascorbic acid per quart

APPROXIMATE YIELD
OF FROZEN FRUITS FROM FRESH

FRUIT	FRESH	FROZEN
Apples	1 bu. (48 lb.)	32 to 40 pt.
	1 box (44 lb.)	29 to 35 pt.
	1¼ to 1½ lb.	1 pt.
Apricots	1 bu. (48 lb.)	60 to 72 pt.
	1 crate (22 lb.)	28 to 33 pt.
	⅔ to ⅘ lb.	1 pt.
*Berries	1 crate (24 qt.)	32 to 36 pt.
	1⅓ to 1½ pt.	1 pt.
Cantaloupe	1 dozen (28 lb.)	22 pt.
	1 to 1¼ lb.	1 pt.
Cherries, sweet or sour	1 bu. (56 lb.)	36 to 44 pt.
	1¼ to 1½ lb.	1 pt.
Cranberries	1 box (25 lb.)	50 pt.
	1 peck (8 lb.)	16 pt.
	½ lb.	1 pt.
Currants	2 qt. (3 lb.)	4 pt.
	¾ lb.	1 pt.
Peaches	1 bu. (48 lb.)	32 to 48 pt.
	1 lug box (20 lb.)	13 to 20 pt.
	1 to 1½ lb.	1 pt.
Pears	1 bu. (50 lb.)	40 to 50 pt.
	1 western box (46 lb.)	37 to 46 pt.
	1 to 1¼ lb.	1 pt.
Pineapple	5 lb.	4 pt.

* Includes blackberries, blueberries, boysenberries, dewberries, elderberries, gooseberries, huckleberries, loganberries, and young-berries.

Plums	1 bu. (56 lb.)	38 to 56 pt.
and prunes	1 crate (20 lb.)	13 to 20 pt.
	1 to 1½ lb.	1 pt.
Raspberries	1 crate (24 pt.)	24 pt.
	1 pt.	1 pt.
Rhubarb	15 lb.	15 to 22 pt.
	⅔ to 1 lb.	1 pt.
Strawberries	1 crate (24 qt.)	38 pt.
	⅔ qt.	1 pt.

40% syrup and pour ½ cup syrup in each pint container and 1 cup in each quart container. Slice peaches directly into syrup-filled containers. Add additional syrup, if needed, to cover peaches, leaving ½-inch headspace for pints and 1-inch headspace for quarts. Crumple waxed paper and place on top of the peaches to hold them under syrup. Seal and freeze.

Sugar pack: Combine sugar with commercial ascorbic acid mixture, following manufacturer's directions, then mix ⅔ cup with each quart prepared peaches. Pack in containers, leaving ½-inch headspace. Seal and freeze.

Pears

Wash, peel, halve or quarter, and core. Heat in boiling 40% syrup 1 to 2 minutes. Drain and cool.

Syrup pack: Pack fruit in containers. Cover cold pears with cold 40% syrup. Leave ½- to 1-inch headspace. Seal and freeze.

Persimmons

Sort, wash, peel, and cut in sections. Press through sieve. Mix each quart persimmon purée with ⅛ teaspoon ascorbic acid.

PEACHES PACKED IN SYRUP

1. Select mature peaches that are firm-ripe with no green color. Allow 1 to 1½ pounds fresh peaches for each pint to be frozen. Wash.

2. For best appearance, pit and peel peaches by hand. They peel more quickly if dipped first in boiling water, but look ragged.

step by step

3. Pour about ½ cup cold syrup into each pint container. Slice peaches directly into container.

4. Add syrup to cover peaches. Leave ½-inch headspace to allow for expansion of the fruit during freezing.

Continued

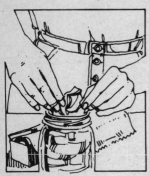 

5. Put crumpled parchment paper over fruit to keep peaches in syrup. It should always cover the fruit to prevent oxidation.

6. Wipe all sealing edges clean for a good seal. Screw lid on tight. Label with name of fruit and date of freezing.

7. Store sealed containers in coldest part of freezer, leaving space so air can circulate. Store at 0°F or below.

Unsweetened: Pack purée in containers, leaving ½- to 1-inch headspace. Seal and freeze.

Sweetened: Mix 1 cup sugar with each quart purée. Pack in containers, leaving ½- to 1-inch headspace. Seal and freeze.

Pineapple

Pare ripe pineapple; remove eyes and core. Slice, dice, crush, or cut in wedges.

Dry pack: Freeze on cookie sheets and pack in containers or bags. Seal and return to freezer.

Syrup pack: Pack fruit in containers and cover with 30% or 40% syrup. Leave ½- to 1-inch headspace. Seal and freeze.

Plums

Sort, wash, halve, and remove pits.

Dry pack: Pack in containers, leaving ½-inch headspace. Seal and freeze. Or freeze on cookie sheets; then pack in bags or containers, seal, and return to freezer.

Syrup pack: Pack fruit in containers. Add ½ teaspoon ascorbic acid to each quart 40% syrup. Use syrup to cover; about 1 cup per quart plums. Leave ½- to 1-inch headspace. Seal and freeze.

Raspberries

Wash in cold water; drain. Avoid overhandling.

Dry pack: Freeze on cookie sheet; then pack or bag, seal, and return to freezer. Or pack lightly in con-

STRAWBERRIES PACKED

1. Select firm, ripe strawberries; about ⅔ quart fresh berries are needed for each pint frozen.

2. Wash berries a few at a time in cold water. Lift them gently out of water and drain.

IN SUGAR step by step

3. Remove hulls. Slice berries into a bowl or shallow pan.

4. Sprinkle sugar (¾ cup to each quart berries) over and turn berries over and over until sugar is dissolved.

Continued

5. Pack berries in container leaving ½-inch headspace. Place crumpled parchment paper over berries to keep them down in juice.

6. Press lid on firmly to seal. Be sure the seal is watertight.

7. Label package with name of fruit and date frozen. Freeze; then store at 0°F or below.

tainers or bags, leaving ½-inch headspace. Seal and freeze.

Sugar pack: Carefully mix ¾ cup sugar with each quart raspberries. Pack in containers, leaving ½-inch headspace. Seal and freeze.

Syrup pack: Pack fruit in containers. Cover with 40% syrup, leaving ½- to 1-inch headspace. Seal and freeze.

Rhubarb

Wash and remove leaves; cut stalks into 1-inch pieces. Blanch in boiling water 1 minute. Chill in cold water; drain.

Dry pack: Freeze on cookie sheets, then pack in bags or containers. Seal and return to freezer. Or pack in containers, leaving ½-inch headspace, seal, and freeze.

Syrup pack: Pack fruit in containers. Cover with 40% syrup, leaving ½- to 1-inch headspace. Seal and freeze.

Strawberries

Wash in cold water; drain. Hull and slice or leave whole.

Unsweetened: Pack whole berries lightly in containers and cover with water (add 1 teaspoon ascorbic acid per quart water). Leave ½- to 1-inch headspace, seal, and freeze.

Dry pack: Freeze small, whole berries on cookie sheet. Pack or bag, seal, and return to freezer.

Sugar pack: Gently mix ½ to ¾ cup sugar with each quart prepared berries. Pack in containers. Leave ½-inch headspace. Seal and freeze.

Syrup pack: Cover medium-sized whole berries with 40% or 50% syrup. Leave ½- to 1-inch headspace. Seal and freeze.

HERBS

Select young, tender leaves of herbs for freezing. Wash in several waters, and blanch in boiling water for 10 seconds. Chill in ice water 1 minute. Pat dry with paper towels.

Seal amounts you use for a single recipe in small plastic bags, in freezer paper, or foil or in plastic wrap. Freeze the individual packages in a labeled larger plastic bag, in paper envelopes, or in rigid plastic containers, or staple all individual packages of the same herb to a labeled piece of cardboard.

Snip herbs right into recipes, just as you would fresh.

Dill: Do not wash. Break heads off stems and place heads in jars. Seal and freeze.

Parsley and chives: Chop as usual, then package amounts you usually use as directed above. Freeze. Use directly from freezer; do not thaw.

 **MEATS**

Freezing is the simplest, safest, quickest, and best way to preserve meat, if you follow the rules. Freezing preserves what you buy, so select and purchase the best you can. With the exception of aged meats, buy the freshest possible.

Freeze meats in package sizes that you use for a meal. For 1- to 2-week storage, just overwrap or overbag store wrappings. For longer storage, unwrap and then rewrap in freezer paper or heavy-duty foil.

Freeze burgers, chops, or steaks on trays or waxed-paper-covered cookie sheets, then package with two sheets of paper between, seal, and return to freezer. Always use moisture-vapor-proof wrappings, wrap and seal following the folding instructions that appear on page 163.

Do not salt or season meat before freezing because it can cause flavor changes.

THAWING

Thawing of frozen meats is not necessary before cooking unless you are using cuts that are to be

    stuffed, molded, or formed
    dredged or coated with crumbs or flour
    deep fried

Thaw meat in wrappings in the refrigerator. A large roast will take 4 to 7 hours per pound. A pound of ground beef or stew meat will take 18 to 20 hours, so plan ahead. To thaw in a microwave oven, follow manufacturer's directions.

Cooking frozen meats is just the same as cooking thawed or fresh meats, only it takes longer. Allow one-third to one-half again as much time to cook a frozen roast.

Broil thick frozen steaks, chops, and ground meat patties slightly further from heat.

Panbroil frozen steaks and chops in a very hot skillet, so meat can brown well before it thaws on surface. (Thawing slows down browning.) When browned, lower the heat and cook, turning meat occasionally so that it can cook to center without browning too much on outside. Some smart cooks buy a lot of ground beef when it's on sale, make some into meat loaves, meat balls, patties, and sauces, then freeze it all.

POULTRY AND GAME

POULTRY

Poultry to go into the freezer should be thoroughly cleaned and all ready to cook just as soon as it comes out. When it is wrapped, labeled, and ready to freeze, put it in the coldest part of the freezer to freeze quickly.

Giblets and livers. Freeze giblets and livers separately on cookie sheets; package or bag, and seal. Use livers within a month, giblets within three months.

Whole birds. Wash whole birds well. Lock wings and fold neck skin over. Push legs down and forward to tie compactly against body of bird. Wrap in moisture-vapor-proof material, fold and seal as described on page 163, or put the bird in a heavy plastic bag. Gently lower the bag into sink of water just until water covers chickens—do not let any water into the bag. The weight of the water will expel all the air from the bag. Twist the bag under water, holding the top of the bag in your other hand, so air cannot get back in. Double twist part of bag and seal with a twist-tie, rubber band, or string.

Poultry should *never* be stuffed and then frozen: it's too dangerous. Stuffing in a bird is a perfect place for bacteria to grow and reproduce. It is safest to prepare and bake stuffing separately. Commercially frozen stuffed poultry has been carefully processed, handled, and inspected, so it is safe to use.

Poultry pieces. Wash bird well and cut into desired pieces. Arrange single layer of pieces on waxed-paper-covered cookie sheet and freeze solid, unwrapped. Package or bag and return to freezer.

Or wrap individual pieces of poultry in plastic wrap; wrap or bag.

Or put pieces in a heavy plastic bag and expel air by lowering into water in sink, as directed on page 214.

Cooked poultry. Cooked poultry can be frozen. For safety's sake, cool the poultry right after cooking. Cut meat from the bones and package in slices or in chunks or pieces. Slices can be frozen in leftover gravy or sauce. Pack in containers or bags (if using bags, expel air as directed on page 214), seal, and freeze.

Thawing poultry. Thaw poultry in wrappings in the refrigerator or, if the package is airtight (a plastic bag, for

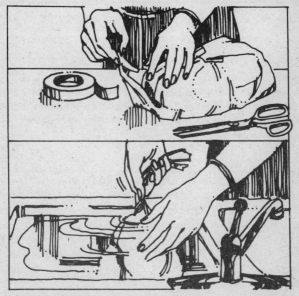

(Top) Wrap bird in moisture-vapor-proof material; fold and seal or (bottom) put in heavy plastic bag; lower in water and twist bag to expel air; tie.

instance), under cold running water. A cut-up fryer will take 10 to 20 hours to refrigerator-thaw, so plan to move it from freezer to refrigerator the night before you want to cook it for supper. (A cut-up fryer will take a couple of hours to thaw under cold running water.) A whole 5-pound bird will take 1 to 2 days to thaw in the refrigerator (4 to 5 hours under cold running water). A large (18+ pound) turkey will take 2 to 3 days to refrigerator-thaw.

To thaw in a microwave oven, follow manufacturer's directions.

Always cook all poultry as soon as it has thawed, but while still extremely cold. Never refreeze uncooked poultry!

Note: You may notice broilers, young fryers, and roasters developing a dark color around the bones when frozen. This is caused by oxidation of bone marrow and is absolutely harmless. It has no effect on flavor or food value.

GAME

Check your state laws to be sure how much game you can store and for what length of time. Game birds are usually handled as for poultry; animals as for meat.

FISH AND SHELLFISH

FISH

Fish is very perishable and its flavor is fleeting, so freeze only the freshest. Prepare it quickly, package properly, and hurry it into the freezer. Clean and prepare fish as if you were going to cook them.

Wrap or bag small, whole fish, seal, and freeze.

Cut larger fish into steaks or fillets and dip in a solution of ⅔ cup salt and a gallon of cold water for 30 seconds. (This firms the fish and reduces leakage or drip when thawed.) Drain well.

Wrap pieces separately in freezer paper, foil, or plastic wrap. Package or bag and seal meal-sized amounts. Put in coldest part of freezer to freeze quickly.

SHELLFISH

Oysters, clams, and scallops. Rinse sand off; remove shells, and save liquor. Wash shellfish in salt brine (1 cup salt and 1 quart cold water); drain. Pack in liquor in cartons or lidded containers, leaving 1-inch headspace. Seal and freeze.

Crabs. Remove back shell of live crabs, eviscerate, and wash. Break in half and cook in boiling water 25 minutes. Cool, then remove meat, keeping body and leg meat separate. Pack in cartons or lidded containers and cover with brine (1 tablespoon salt and 1 quart water). Leave 1-inch headspace. Seal and freeze.

Lobster. Drop live into boiling salted water and cook 20 minutes. Cool lobsters on their backs. Remove meat

Prepare fish as for cooking. Dip big pieces in salt water; wrap and seal.

from shells. Pack in cartons or lidded containers, leaving 1-inch headspace. Seal and freeze.

Shrimp. Remove heads, peel, and clean, or remove heads and back veins and leave in shell. Wash thoroughly. Spread out on waxed-paper-covered cookie sheets and freeze solid. Package or bag, seal, and return to freezer. Do not freeze cooked shrimp—they get tough during freezer storage.

THAWING

Thaw fish and shellfish in package or wrapping, in the refrigerator for 8 to 10 hours for a 1-pound package. Cook immediately. Never refreeze fish.

 # DAIRY PRODUCTS

Most dairy products freeze well—only a few do not take to the freezer. Sour cream, yogurt, and the like lose their creamy texture, but give them a spin in the blender and they'll be smooth again. Creamed cottage cheese gets mushy, although dry cottage cheese freezes well. Whipping cream does not whip to as great volume if it has been frozen. Whip first, then freeze (see page 221).

MILK

Although milk does not look or taste as good after it has been frozen, many cooks like to keep some on hand in the freezer for emergencies. (Others keep nonfat dry milk on a cupboard shelf.) Thaw milk in the refrigerator.

BUTTER

Overwrap original wrapping or bag and seal to protect the flavor of butter. If desired, buy butter for freezing when the price is good. Fancy butters—curls, balls, etc. —can be wrapped or bagged, sealed, and frozen.

CHEESE

The dairy people used to recommend that cheese not be frozen. But so many homemakers did it anyway that the experts decided to make this suggestion: cut cheese in pieces about 1 inch thick and no more than ½ pound each. Wrap tightly in heavy-duty foil or freezer paper and freeze. Thaw in the refrigerator, in the wrappings and use as soon as possible after thawing. Frozen cheese will be crumblier than unfrozen, and the surface of the cheese may be slightly mottled from moisture. Flavor is just as good, however, and even better if you let cheese come to room temperature before serving. Cream cheese can be frozen, too. Just overwrap.

CREAM

Whip heavy cream until stiff, sweeten, and drop dollops on a waxed-paper-covered baking sheet. Freeze solid, then bag or pack layers, with paper between, in rigid containers. Seal and return to freezer. Place dollop on dessert and let stand just a few minutes to thaw before serving.

ICE CREAM
(and all its kind)

Freeze ice cream and related products just as it comes from the store. After opening, cover the scooped part of the ice cream with a piece of freezer paper or plastic. Some cooks prefer to keep containers of ice cream in a plastic bag or special-size rigid plastic container to help prevent crystallization.

Let ice cream stand at room temperature just a few minutes for easier scooping.

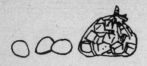 **EGGS**

Farm folk, big bakers, and smart shoppers like to freeze eggs when they are plentiful and cheap. You can freeze eggs as yolks, as whites, or whole. Take a moment to think how you most often use them, then pack and freeze accordingly. Do not freeze eggs in the shell because they'll crack. And do not freeze hard-cooked eggs because they get rubbery and tough. Never refreeze eggs. Once thawed, they must be used.

WHOLE EGGS

To freeze whole eggs, carefully break eggs, one at a time, and check carefully for freshness and quality and for bits of shell. Use only the best. Gently mix but do not beat, because you don't want any air bubbles. Pressing through a sieve or food mill does the mixing nicely. For dessert use, add 1½ teaspoons sugar or corn syrup for each cup of eggs. For other uses add ½ teaspoon salt per cup of eggs. Freeze in amounts you ordinarily need. For example, 2 eggs for cake mixes, cakes, and cookies; 3 eggs for omelets; 6 eggs to scramble for breakfast. Use small plastic containers or plastic sandwich bags (double), or you can freeze eggs in ice cube trays for convenient egg blocks. Pour water into each cube compartment and measure the amount of water for each cube. 2½ tablespoons equals 1 whole egg, so small cube compartments may hold only half an egg. Allow room for expansion during freezing. Pour eggs into ice cube trays and freeze, unwrapped, until solid. Then transfer to plastic bag, seal and freeze.

EGG YOLKS

To prepare egg yolks for freezing, first separate the eggs. Press the yolks through a sieve or food mill. Stir in ½ teaspoon salt or 1½ teaspoons sugar or corn syrup for each cup of yolks. Freeze in amounts needed for individual recipes, measuring 1 tablespoon to equal 1 yolk. Freeze in ice cube tray, small plastic containers, or doubled plastic sandwich bags. If using ice cube trays, freeze yolks solid, then remove, package or bag, seal, and return to freezer.

EGG WHITES

To freeze egg whites, separate the eggs, then press the whites through a sieve or food mill. Avoid adding any air bubbles. Measure 1½ tablespoons to equal 1 white, and freeze in amounts needed for recipes. You can freeze measured amounts such as 1 cup for angel or chiffon cakes. Check your favorite recipe for the exact amount. Package in containers or bags, or freeze solid in ice cube trays and then bag or package and return to freezer. Frozen, thawed whites whip just as well as fresh.

THAWING

Thaw whole eggs, egg yolks, and egg whites in unopened container in the refrigerator or at room temperature. Thaw cubes in a small bowl, covered with plastic wrap, in the refrigerator. Use thawed whole eggs and yolks as soon as possible. Thawed whites can be refrigerated for a day or two. Remember that sugar or salt has been added to whole eggs and egg yolks and adjust the recipe you use accordingly.

 # SANDWICHES

Every lunch packer dreams of the morning when she won't have to make sandwiches. With a freezer, you can prepare a week's worth of sandwiches at once. Come morning all you do is move them from freezer to a lunch box or bag. By lunchtime they'll be thawed.

Some typical sandwich fillings do not freeze well. Mayonnaise separates, lettuce, celery, and other crisp foods go limp, hard-cooked eggs get tough. You can always pack these foods separately, to be tucked in or spread on sandwiches just before they are eaten.

Lots of sandwich favorites DO freeze well—peanut butter; sliced, diced or ground cooked chicken; meat or fish; chopped nuts; dried chopped fruit; chopped or sliced olives; crushed pineapple; cheese. Use bottled salad dressing, cream cheese, sour cream, milk, lemon, orange or pineapple juice, or applesauce to hold ingredients together in place of mayonnaise.

When preparing sandwiches, always spread bread slices with softened butter, right to the edges. This seals bread and keeps the filling from soaking in. For extra zip, mix a little horseradish, mustard, chili sauce, or even a pinch of herbs into the butter for spreading.

Wrap each sandwich separately in freezer paper, heavy-duty foil or plastic wrap, and seal. If using plastic sandwich bags, be sure to seal them with tape. Label and freeze. Two weeks is maximum freezer time for most sandwiches.

THAWING

Pack frozen sandwiches in lunch boxes and they will thaw by noon. At home, thaw at room temperature about 3 hours. Keep thawed sandwiches in the refrigerator until ready to serve.

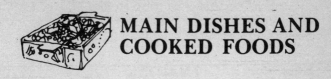 # MAIN DISHES AND COOKED FOODS

There are lots of good things in life and one of them is coming home at the end of a long day, taking a main dish out of the freezer, and letting the oven do the work. With a freezer at hand you can cook when you feel like it, doubling or tripling a recipe, and freeze meal-sized amounts. (The recipes that follow are great freeze-aheads.) When preparing dishes for freezing, do not use hard-cooked egg whites because they get tough if frozen. Use seasonings sparingly, since some tend to get stronger in the freezer. It's best to season when ready to reheat.

Sauces and gravies may separate when reheated after freezing. Use less fat in preparation and stir while reheating.

Canned condensed soups are the best base for creamed dishes because they do not separate. Potatoes can get mushy in stews or meat pies, for example. Stir them in just before serving.

If you are going to cook foods before freezing, always undercook them. The reheating will finish the cooking. This is especially important for fried foods —cook just until barely brown. Cool food quickly before freezing. Put the pan in the sink or other large pan of ice water to cool down. Stir occasionally to help it along.

Freeze the food right in casseroles or baking dishes, or use aluminum pans. You can line a casserole or baking dish with foil, fill with food, freeze solid, and then lift out the food in the foil to overwrap or bag. Then you have a casserole to use, not to freeze.

Package foods in amounts that your family will use for one meal.

Food may be packed in cartons or lidded containers, if you wish. Remember to leave an inch of headspace for expansion.

Never refreeze frozen, reheated foods.

THAWING

Most foods can be reheated without thawing, in a saucepan, double boiler, in the oven, or in a microwave oven. Top-of-range reheating must be done over low heat, with frequent stirring to prevent sticking or burning. Foil pans can go right into the oven. Casserole shaped foods in foil can go right back into the casserole or baking dish they were frozen in. Cover until the food is thawed, then remove cover near the end of cooking time to brown the food. If the dish you're using does not have a cover, just use aluminum foil, with the dull side up. The dull side absorbs more heat than the shiny side.

Reheating takes less time if foods have been almost thoroughly cooked before freezing. Of course, thawed foods reheat more quickly than still-frozen foods.

 # BAKED GOODS

Your freezer can store baked goods beautifully, letting you stock up on bread when the price is right, and giving you the freedom to bake a lot when you feel like it without worrying about the surplus getting stale. And you will always have something on hand for family as well as planned or unplanned company.

Only a few baked products do not take well to the freezer—meringue and custard pies, cakes with soft fillings, egg white frostings. Otherwise, anything goes. Just take a look at all the commercially frozen baked items in your supermarket and you'll realize how very many breads, doughs, cakes, cookies, pastries, and other baked goods can be stored in the freezer.

YEAST BREADS

Bakery or store bread can wait a week in the freezer in the plastic bag it comes in. For storage longer than that (and only a week or so more is recommended), over-wrap or put in another plastic bag. To thaw, let stand in the bag at room temperature for about ½ hour. You can make lunch-box sandwiches with frozen bread because it will have thawed by noon.

Homemade yeast breads can be baked, cooled, then frozen solid, unwrapped. When frozen, wrap or put in a plastic bag and seal. To thaw, let stand in bag or wrapper at room temperature about ½ hour. To serve warm, take the loaf out of the bag or wrapper, brush the top with melted butter, and heat in 350°F oven about 10 to 15 minutes. If loaf is wrapped in foil, heat right in wrappings.

Rolls, coffee cakes, and similar items should be handled just as yeast breads. Bake, cool, and freeze solid, unwrapped. When frozen, wrap or put in a plastic bag

and seal. To thaw, let stand at room temperature or
unwrap and warm in a 350°F oven for 5 to 10 minutes,
depending on the size of the bread. Coffee cakes are
better frozen unfrosted. Frost them, if you wish, just
before serving.

QUICK BREADS

Bake and cool quick breads, and freeze solid, unwrapped. Then wrap or bag and seal. Popovers, muffins,
cornbread, waffles, fruit and nut breads—they all freeze
just fine. Thaw as for rolls and coffee cakes. Waffles,
pancakes, and French toast can be made when you have
plenty of time, frozen solid, then packed or bagged.
Just drop in the toaster to thaw on hurried mornings.

DOUGHS

Some doughs can be frozen before baking. You can
mix, roll, and cut biscuits, freeze solid, and then bag
and seal to bake whenever you wish. Bake thawed or
unthawed, remembering to increase baking time for unthawed biscuits. Frozen yeast doughs are best prepared
from specially formulated recipes (see pages 234-240).

CAKES

Cakes can be frozen either iced or uniced. To prepare
cakes for freezer-storage, first bake and cool.

Uniced cakes should be frozen solid, then wrapped
or bagged, sealed, and put back in the freezer. To thaw
uniced cakes, let stand in wrapping at room temperature
for an hour, or in a 300°F oven for about 10 minutes.

Iced cakes should be frozen, unwrapped, so the wrapping won't stick to the icing. Butter frostings are best
for freezing. To thaw iced cakes, unwrap or unbag, then
cover with a tall cake cover, bowl, or pan that does not
touch top of cake. Let stand at room temperature about
an hour. Covering the iced cake as it thaws prevents
beads of liquid from forming on the icing as it thaws.

Cupcakes, loaf cakes, and tube cakes get the same treatment as layers. Cupcakes thaw in less time than layers, loaf and tube cakes take longer.

COOKIES

Many a Christmas cookie maker starts her holiday baking early in November and stashes each batch away in the freezer. One smart cook, with many children, carefully labels the cookies she wants saved as "liver."

Baked cookies should be frozen, then carefully packed in rigid containers to prevent breaking or crumbling. Thaw, in wrappers or containers, at room temperature.

Cookie dough can be made whenever you have the time. Freeze rolled or drop cookie dough in a ball or roll; thaw at room temperature. Roll up dough for refrigerator cookies as usual, wrap and seal. Slice and bake as many as you want, whenever you want.

You may also roll out cookie dough, cut shapes, and stack in layers, separated by sheets of freezer wrap or waxed paper, and freeze until ready to bake.

Prepare drop cookies similarly: mix dough, drop by spoonfuls ¼ inch apart on cookie sheets, freeze firm, then package with double sheets of waxed or freezer paper between each layer of drops. Just plop drops on cookie sheet and put right into the oven to bake.

PIES AND PASTRY

When you feel like baking, bake a lot. What a pleasure to serve hot homemade cherry pie on a day when you haven't been near the kitchen!

Fruit and berry pies are better if frozen before baking—this keeps their crusts crispier. But all pies (with the exception of cream, custard, and meringue pies, which shouldn't be frozen at all) can be frozen baked or unbaked.

Baked pies should be baked, cooled, and frozen in the pie plate until solid. Wrap or bag, seal, and return to freezer. Thaw at room temperature, in wrappings. Then unwrap and heat in a 350°F oven for about 20 minutes.

Unbaked pies should also be frozen in the pie plate, unwrapped. Bag or wrap, seal, and return to freezer.

Fruit and mince pies freeze best if the inside of the pie pan is brushed with a coating of 2 parts shortening creamed with 1 part flour. Or brush the bottom crust with melted butter or slightly beaten egg white. This keeps the crust from getting soggy. Prepare recipe as usual. Tapioca is a better thickener than cornstarch for freezer fruit pies.

Chiffon pies can be frozen solid before wrapping, so wrapping won't stick to the filling.

Pumpkin pie can be baked, cooled, and frozen, then wrapped. Or you can freeze the filling separately, thaw, pour into unbaked pastry, and bake.

Pack frozen pies carefully. Covering the top with an inverted paper plate helps protect the top crust. Set aside a safe corner of the freezer for pies, where they are not likely to get bumped or stacked upon.

Pastry and pie crust can be prepared when you're in the mood and frozen in balls or rounds. With 2 sheets of waxed or freezer paper between each flat round, stack the rolled pastry on a cookie sheet and freeze solid. Carefully slip the frozen rounds into a rigid container (bakery box, large plastic pie carrier, etc.) for safe storage and keep in the freezer. Let the pastry rounds stand at room temperature until thawed, about 10 minutes. Ease into pie pan and proceed as usual.

FROZEN DINNERS

Your kitchen can become a convenience food factory with absolutely no effort on your part. When you have just a serving of everything left over at the end of a meal, don't carefully package the dibs and dabs to die a lingering death in the refrigerator. Just arrange meat, vegetables, potatoes, etc. on divided foil trays, cover tightly with foil, label, and freeze. Save the trays from commercially frozen dinners, or you can even buy divided aluminum trays.

Just imagine—a week of dinner leftovers can equal seven stashed-away dinners! Clever freezer-cooks often cook more than enough of family favorite meals just so they can freeze tray dinners. There's a special secure feeling that comes from knowing that you can arrive home at 6 and still have a full meal on the table at 6:30, or knowing that you can dine out while still leaving a good, hot meal for the stay-at-homes, or that you can please a finicky eater with a meal just for him.

There are a few tricks for tray dinner success:

Cover sliced meats with gravy or sauce so they won't dry out when reheated. Fried foods need no sauce or gravy coating.

Butter vegetables so they will stay moist.

Fill foil trays as you serve dinner and let them cool in the refrigerator while you eat. After dinner, cover the trays tightly with foil, seal, label, and freeze. Don't forget to add the trays to your freezer inventory.

Heat tray dinners in a 375°F oven for about 35 to 45 minutes. The total time depends on the foods you've frozen. Uncover fried foods after 20 minutes of heating so they can brown and crisp.

Include heating directions on the label.

If trays aren't your thing, you can still freeze leftovers (plan-aheads is today's word for them). Wrap individual foods in foil or freezer paper or pack in plastic or boilable bags or containers and label, then freeze. Some cooks package the components of an entire meal separately, then stash the whole meal in a plastic bag and label it with heating instructions for each item, including times, temperatures, and pans. You can do a week's worth of dinners like this, even numbering or marking the meal bags for the day of the week. Mothers who are going to be away from home for several days can make up daily menus, indicating a meal bag for each day along with refrigerator or shelf items needed to round out the meal.

The best food combinations to freeze for tray or freeze-ahead dinners are those that your family likes best. If you're on the lookout for combinations, try any of the following, or take a look at the commercially frozen dinners to see what combinations they put forth.

Meat loaf with gravy or tomato sauce, whipped potatoes, green beans.

Ham slices with raisin sauce, candied sweet potatoes, buttered peas.

Roast beef with mushroom sauce, baked potatoes, Brussels sprouts.

Fried chicken, french fried potatoes, corn.

Turkey with giblet gravy, dressing, broccoli.

Roast pork slices with applesauce, whipped sweet potatoes or brown rice, Italian green beans.

Beef patties with chili sauce, steamed rice, whipped acorn squash.

Don't try to duplicate everything you see packed in commercially frozen dinners. Puddings, for example, are specially formulated to withstand freezing and reheating. Homemade puddings can't go through that without separating. Fruit crisps and sauces will freeze and reheat well.

Flour and egg thickened sauces will separate when

frozen and reheated, and some will curdle. But they will be safe to eat and will taste just as good when reheated. Sometimes stirring just after heating will help restore good looks to creamed dishes. Macaroni and cheese, scalloped chicken, chicken à la king, and beef stroganoff are all candidates for frozen dinner main dishes. Remember to slightly undercook any pasta product (macaroni, noodles, spaghetti) that will accompany them. The pasta will finish cooking during the reheating.

If you are lucky enough to own a microwave oven, you will want to package your frozen dinners in something other than aluminum trays; check your microwave oven use and care booklet for more information about packaging. Paper or plastic plates are your best bet. Again, check your oven manual for how to arrange foods for best reheating.

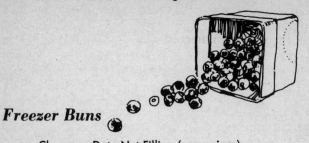

Freezer Buns

Cheese or Date-Nut Filling (see recipes)
5¼ to 6¼ cups unsifted flour
⅓ cup sugar
1 teaspoon salt
½ teaspoon grated lemon peel
2 packages active dry yeast
1 cup softened margarine
1⅓ cups very warm tap water (120-130°F)
2 eggs (at room temperature)
Confectioners' sugar

1. Prepare desired filling. Refrigerate until ready to use.
2. Mix 1½ cups flour, sugar, salt, lemon peel, and undissolved yeast thoroughly in a large bowl. Add margarine.
3. Add tap water gradually to dry ingredients and beat 2 minutes at medium speed of electric mixer, scraping bowl occasionally. Add eggs and ½ cup flour. Beat at high speed 2 minutes, scraping bowl occasionally. Stir in enough additional flour to make a soft dough. Cover; let rest 20 minutes.
4. Turn dough out onto a well floured board. Divide into 3 equal pieces. Roll each piece into an 8-inch square. Cut each into eight 1-inch strips. Twist each strip and coil into a circle, sealing ends underneath. Place on greased baking sheets. Make wide indentations in center of each coil, pressing to bottom. Spoon prepared filling into indentations, using about 2 tablespoons Cheese Filling or 1 tablespoon Date-Nut Filling for each roll. Cover loosely with plastic wrap. Freeze

until firm. Transfer to plastic bags. Freeze up to 4 weeks.

5. Remove from freezer; place on ungreased baking sheets. Cover loosely with plastic wrap. Let stand at room temperature until fully thawed, about 1 hour and 45 minutes. Let rise in warm place, free from draft, until more than doubled in bulk, about 45 minutes.

6. Bake at 375°F 15 to 20 minutes, or until evenly browned. Remove from baking sheets and cool on wire racks. Sprinkle with confectioners' sugar.

About 2 dozen buns

Cheese Filling

Blend **2 packages (8 ounces each) cream cheese**, softened, **1/2 cup sugar**, and **1 tablespoon grated lemon peel.** Add **2 egg whites** gradually, blending until smooth.

Date-Nut Filling

Bring **2 cups pitted dates** and **1/2 cup water** to boiling in a saucepan. Reduce heat; cover and simmer until water is absorbed, about 3 minutes. Stir in **1/2 cup chopped walnuts.**

Blueberry Coconut Parfait

2 cups dairy sour cream
⅓ cup sugar
1 teaspoon vanilla extract
½ teaspoon ground mace
2 teaspoons grated orange peel
½ cup flaked coconut
4 cups fresh or dry-pack frozen blueberries

1. Mix sour cream, sugar, vanilla extract, mace, orange peel, and coconut.

2. Spoon alternating layers of sour cream mixture and blueberries into parfait glasses beginning and ending

with sour cream mixture. Garnish top with additional blueberries.

6 servings

Mixed Fruit Salad with Mayonnaise

1 cup each canned apricot and peach halves
1 cup canned pineapple chunks
½ cup syrup (drained from canned fruit)
1 envelope unflavored gelatin
½ cup sugar
3 tablespoons lemon juice
¼ cup sliced maraschino cherries
1 cup chilled whipping cream
1 cup mayonnaise

1. Cut apricots, peaches, and pineapple into ½-inch pieces. Put into a large bowl. Measure syrup.
2. Mix gelatin and sugar thoroughly in a saucepan. Blend in syrup. Stir over low heat until gelatin is dissolved. Cool slightly.
3. Turn gelatin into bowl and mix in lemon juice and cherries. Blend well and chill until slightly thickened.
4. Beat whipping cream until soft peaks are formed. Continue beating while blending in mayonnaise. Mix thoroughly with fruit mixture.
5. *To freeze:* Spoon salad into two 1-pint round freezer cartons or a 1-quart mold. Seal tightly and freeze.
6. *To serve:* Remove cartons or mold from freezer about ½ hour before serving time and set in refrigerator until salad is just firm enough to slice. Remove from cartons or unmold. Cut into ¾-inch crosswise slices and serve on **crisp salad greens.**

About 8 servings

Freezer White Bread

    12½ to 13½ cups unsifted flour
      ½ cup sugar
      ⅔ cup instant nonfat dry milk solids
      2 tablespoons salt
      4 packages active dry yeast
      ¼ cup (½ stick) softened margarine
      4 cups very warm tap water (120° to 130°F)

1. In large bowl thoroughly mix 4 cups flour, sugar, dry milk solids, salt, and undissolved dry yeast. Add margarine.

2. Gradually add tap water to dry ingredients and beat 2 minutes at medium speed of electric mixer, scraping bowl occasionally. Add 1½ cups flour. Beat at high speed 2 minutes. Stir in enough additional flour to make a stiff dough.

3. Turn out on lightly floured board; knead until smooth and elastic, about 15 minutes. Cover with a towel; let rest 15 minutes.

4. Divide dough into 4 equal pieces. Form each piece into a smooth round ball. Flatten each ball into a mound 6 inches in diameter. Place on greased baking sheets. Cover with plastic wrap. Freeze until firm. Transfer to plastic bags. Freeze up to 4 weeks.

5. To bake, remove from freezer; place on ungreased baking sheets. Cover; let stand at room temperature until fully thawed, about 4 hours.

6. Roll each ball into a 12 × 8-inch rectangle. Roll up towards you beginning with upper short side. Seal edges and ends, folding sealed ends under. Place loaves in greased 8½ × 4½ × 2½-inch loaf pans. Let rise in warm place until doubled in bulk, about 1½ hours.

7. Bake at 350°F about 35 minutes, or until done. Remove from pans and cool on wire racks.

4 loaves bread

Freezer Pecan Sticky Buns

Pecan sticky syrup:
    ½ cup (1 stick) margarine
    1 cup packed dark brown sugar
    ½ cup light corn syrup
    1 cup broken pecans

Buns:
    5½ to 6½ cups unsifted flour
    ¾ cup sugar
    1 teaspoon salt
    3 packages active dry yeast
    ½ cup (1 stick) margarine, softened
    1 cup very warm tap water (120° to 130°F)
    3 eggs (at room temperature)
    Melted margarine
    ½ cup packed dark brown sugar

1. Melt margarine; stir in brown sugar and corn syrup. Heat, stirring, until sugar is dissolved. Pour into 2 greased 9-inch square pans. Sprinkle each pan with ½ cup pecans. Set pans aside.

2. Thoroughly mix 1¼ cups flour, sugar, salt, and undissolved yeast. Add margarine. Gradually add tap water and beat 2 minutes at medium speed of electric mixer, scraping bowl occasionally. Add eggs and ¼ cup flour. Beat at high speed 2 minutes, scraping bowl occasionally. Stir in enough additional flour to make a soft dough.

3. Turn out on lightly floured board; knead until smooth and elastic, about 8 to 10 minutes. Divide dough in half. Roll one half into a 14 × 9-inch rectangle. Brush with melted margarine; sprinkle with half the brown sugar. Roll up from short end to form a roll 9 inches long. Pinch seam to seal. Cut into nine 1-inch slices. Arrange cut side up in a prepared pan. Cover pan tightly with plastic wrap, then aluminum foil;

freeze. Repeat with remaining dough and brown sugar. Keep frozen up to 4 weeks.

4. To bake, let stand, covered with plastic wrap, at room temperature until fully thawed, about 3 hours. Let rise in warm place, free from draft, until more than doubled in bulk, about 1 hour and 15 minutes.

5. Bake at 375°F 20 to 25 minutes, or until done. Cool 10 minutes in pan. Invert rolls onto plates to cool.

1½ dozen buns

Freezer Crumb Cake

    Crumb Topping (see recipe)
5½ to 6½ cups unsifted flour
  ¾ cup sugar
   1 teaspoon salt
   3 packages active dry yeast
  ½ cup softened margarine
   1 cup very warm tap water (120-130°F)
   3 eggs (at room temperature)
   Melted margarine

1. Prepare Crumb Topping. Refrigerate until ready to use.

2. Mix 1¼ cups flour, sugar, salt, and undissolved active dry yeast thoroughly in a large bowl. Add margarine.

3. Add tap water gradually to dry ingredients and beat 2 minutes at medium speed of electric mixer, scraping bowl occasionally. Add eggs and ¼ cup flour. Beat at high speed 2 minutes, scraping bowl occasionally. Stir in enough additional flour to make a soft dough. Turn out onto lightly floured board; knead until smooth and elastic, about 8 to 10 minutes.

4. Divide dough into 3 equal pieces. Roll one piece into an 8-inch square. Press into a greased 8-inch square baking pan. Brush with melted margarine. Sprinkle with a third of prepared Crumb Topping. Cover pan tightly with plastic wrap, then with aluminum foil; place in

freezer. Repeat with remaining dough and topping. Keep frozen up to 6 weeks.

5. Remove from freezer. Let stand, covered with plastic wrap, at room temperature until fully thawed, about 3½ hours. Let rise in a warm place, free from draft, until more than doubled in bulk, about 1½ hours.

6. Bake at 375°F about 25 minutes, or until done. Remove from baking pans and cool on wire racks. If desired, sprinkle with confectioners' sugar.

Three 8-inch square cakes

Crumb Topping

Blend **3/4 cup all-purpose flour, 1/3 cup sugar,** and **1 1/2 teaspoons ground cinnamon.** Mix in **6 tablespoons margarine** just until mixture is crumbly.

Blueberry Sugar Cakes

½ cup shortening
1 cup sugar
½ teaspoon salt
3 eggs
2 cups all-purpose flour
2 teaspoons baking powder
1 cup milk
¾ cup fresh or dry-pack frozen blueberries

1. Put shortening, sugar, and salt into a large bowl; work with a wooden spoon until well blended. Stir in eggs.

2. Sift flour and baking powder together and add to mixture. Add milk gradually and beat mixture for 60

strokes until dough is smooth and satiny. Carefully fold in blueberries.

3. Spoon batter into well-greased muffin-pan wells.

4. Bake at 400°F about 15 to 20 minutes, or until wooden pick comes out clean.

About 15 cakes

Blueberry Pie

Crust:
> 2 cups all-purpose flour
> ¼ teaspoon salt
> 2 teaspoons sugar
> ¾ cup shortening
> 5 tablespoons ice water

Filling:
> 1 quart dry-pack frozen blueberries
> 1 cup sugar
> ¾ cup cold water
> 1 tablespoon lemon juice
> 3 tablespoons cornstarch

1. For crust, mix dry ingredients in a bowl and cut in shortening using 2 knives or a pastry blender. Add water, 1 tablespoon at a time, mixing after each addition.

2. Roll into a ball and refrigerate 1 hour before using.

3. For filling, wash and drain blueberries. Put into a saucepan and add sugar, ½ cup water, and lemon juice; bring to boiling over low heat.

4. Dissolve cornstarch in remaining ¼ cup water. As soon as blueberry mixture comes to boiling, stir in cornstarch and remove from heat. Set aside to cool.

5. Roll out pastry for top and bottom pie crusts. Line a 9-inch pie plate with crust, pour in filling, and cover with top crust, pressing down edges and perforating top.

6. Bake at 400°F about 15 to 20 minutes, or until crust is browned.

One 9-inch pie

Freezer Bran Muffins

    3 cups whole bran cereal
    1 cup boiling water
    ½ cup shortening
 1½ cups sugar
    2 eggs
    2 cups buttermilk
    3 cups sifted all-purpose flour
 2½ teaspoons baking soda
    ½ teaspoon salt

1. Put bran cereal into a bowl. Pour in boiling water. Set aside until cool.
2. Put shortening and sugar into a large mixer bowl. Beat until thoroughly blended. Beat in eggs one at a time. Alternately mix in the soaked bran and buttermilk.
3. Sift flour, baking soda, and salt together; add to the bran mixture and mix gently until ingredients are thoroughly moistened (do not overmix).
4. *To freeze batter:* Pour batter into jars or other containers (leave headspace), cover tightly and place in freezer for up to 6 weeks.
5. *To thaw batter:* Remove jars from freezer and thaw in the refrigerator or at room temperature *only* until batter is of pouring consistency.
6. Pour batter into well-greased 2- to 2½-inch muffin-pan wells, filling each about ⅔ full.
7. Bake at 400°F 15 to 18 minutes, or until muffins test done.

About 3 dozen muffins

Note: The batter may be stored, tightly covered, in the refrigerator up to 3 weeks, instead of being frozen. When ready to use, remove the batter from refrigerator and immediately pour into greased muffin-pan wells and bake.

Variations: **Chopped raisins, dates,** or **nuts** (about ½ cup for each quart of batter) may be folded into batter before pouring into muffin wells.

Deep-Dish Apple Pie

  Cheese Pastry Topping (see recipe)
 ¾ cup firmly packed brown sugar
 3 tablespoons flour
 1 teaspoon ground cinnamon
 ¼ teaspoon ground nutmeg
 ½ teaspoon salt
 3 tablespoons butter or margarine
 1 teaspoon grated orange peel
 6 to 7 medium firm tart apples (6 cups, sliced)
 ¼ cup orange juice
 1 tablespoon lemon juice

1. Prepare pastry and set aside.
2. Mix brown sugar, flour, spices, and salt thoroughly. Add butter and orange peel. Cut in with pastry blender or 2 knives until mixture is in coarse crumbs.
3. Wash, quarter, core, pare, and cut apples into ⅛-inch slices. Put apples into a bowl and drizzle orange and lemon juices over them. Gently turn apples with a fork to coat with juice.

4. Arrange one half of apple slices in a 1½-quart deep casserole. Sprinkle with one half of sugar mixture; repeat. Arrange Cheese Pastry Topping on casserole and flute edge. Proceed as desired.

6 to 8 servings

To freeze unbaked pie and serve: Wrap unbaked pie and seal tightly. To protect crust, set package in a pasteboard box or encircle with pasteboard collar. Label and place in freezer. When ready to bake, remove wrappings and carefully cut slits in crust. Bake at 450°F 15 to 20 minutes. Turn oven control to 375°F and bake 25 to 35 minutes, or until crust is golden and apples are tender. Serve warm.

To freeze baked pie and serve: Bake at 450°F 10 minutes. Turn oven control to 350°F and bake 25 to 30 minutes longer, or until apples are tender and crust is golden. Cool completely, wrap and package for freezer as directed for unbaked pie. To thaw, remove wrappings and loosely cover top of pie with aluminum foil. Set in a 325°F oven 35 to 40 minutes, or just long enough to thaw and heat to serving temperature.

To complete without freezing: Bake pie as directed. If desired, serve accompanied with cream, ice cream, sweetened whipped cream, or whipped dessert topping.

Cheese Pastry Topping

1 cup sifted all-purpose flour
½ teaspoon salt
3 tablespoons lard, vegetable shortening, or
    all-purpose shortening
¾ cup shredded sharp Cheddar cheese
2 to 3 tablespoons cold water

1. Mix flour and salt in a bowl. Add lard and cheese;

cut in with a pastry blender or 2 knives until pieces are the size of small peas.

2. Sprinkle cold water gradually over mixture, about a tablespoonful at a time, mixing lightly with a fork after each addition. Add only enough water to hold pastry together. Work quickly; do not overhandle. Shape into a ball and flatten on lightly floured surface.

3. Roll dough to about ⅛-inch thickness and about 1 inch larger than overall size of casserole or pie pan top. Cut a design in pastry to allow steam to escape during baking. (Omit slit design if pie or casserole is to be frozen unbaked.)

4. Place pastry on mixture in casserole or pie pan and fold overhang under; flute or press edge with a fork. Bake as directed.

1 pastry topping for casserole or pie

Cheese Meat Macaroni Casserole

Casserole mixture:
- 8 ounces (2 cups) elbow macaroni
- 2 tablespoons butter or margarine
- 2 tablespoons flour
- ½ teaspoon salt
- Few grains pepper
- ¼ teaspoon dry mustard
- ¼ teaspoon paprika
- 2 cups milk
- 6 ounces sharp Cheddar cheese, shredded (about 1½ cups)
- ½ cup finely chopped onion
- 1 teaspoon Worcestershire sauce

Topping:
- Tomato, about 16 thin slices
- Luncheon meat (12-ounce can), cut crosswise into 14 slices
- Process sharp Cheddar cheese, 8 slices (8 ounces), cut diagonally in halves
- Melted butter or margarine

1. Cook macaroni, following package directions. Drain and set aside.

2. Heat butter in a saucepan. Stir in flour, salt, pepper, dry mustard, and paprika. Heat and stir until bubbly. Add milk gradually, stirring until smooth. Cook and stir until mixture comes to boiling. Remove from heat and mix in cheese, onion, and Worcestershire sauce. Stir until thoroughly blended.

3. Turn one half of the macaroni into a greased 2-quart casserole or baking dish and cover with one half of cheese sauce. Repeat layers.

4. *To freeze:* Cool casserole, wrap in aluminum foil, and place in freezer.

5. *To serve:* Place wrapped casserole in a 350°F oven about 40 minutes, or until thawed. Remove wrapping; cover entire top of macaroni mixture with overlapping slices of tomato, luncheon meat, and cheese. Lightly brush with melted butter. Return to oven and continue heating until casserole mixture is very hot and cheese slices are softened and tinged with brown.

About 8 servings

INDEX